THEATREWRITINGS

THEATRE

PERFORMING ARTS JOURNAL PUBLICATIONS

NEW YORK

WRITINGS

BONNIE
MARRANCA

"Art works clearly are superior to
all other things; since they stay longer
in the world than anything else, they
are the worldliness of all things."

Hannah Arendt

for Gautam, his presence of mind

by Bonnie Marranca

Theatrewritings
American Playwrights (with Gautam Dasgupta)

as Editor

The Theatre of Images
American Dreams: The Imagination of Sam Shepard
Animations: A Trilogy for Mabou Mines
Theatre of the Ridiculous

Acknowledgements

Performing Arts Journal first published "Alphabetical Shepard" in PAJ 14, Vol. V, No. 2 (1981); "The Self as Text" in PAJ 10/11, Vol. IV, Nos. 1 & 2 (1979); "The Real Life of Maria Irene Fornes" in PAJ 22, Vol. VIII, No. 1 (1984); "The Archaeology of Consciousness" in PAJ 12, Vol. IV, No. 3 (1980); "The Politics of Performance" in PAJ 16, Vol. VI, No. 1 (1981); "Pirandello: A Work in Progress" in PAJ 20, Vol. VII, No. 2 (1983).

LIVE Magazine first published "Our Town Our Country" and "Performance/ Art/Theatre" (originally titled "Soho's Bourgeois Gentilhomme: Douglas Davis") in LIVE 6/7 (1982).

"Peter Handke's *My Foot My Tutor*" was published in the *Michigan Quarterly Review*, Vol. XVI, No. 3 (Summer, 1977).

"The Theatre of Images: An Introduction" and "The Ontological-Hysteric Theater of Richard Foreman" are from *The Theatre of Images*, copyright 1977 Bonnie Marranca, reprinted by permission of the Publisher, Drama Book Publishers, New York.

"Robert Wilson, the Avant-Garde and the Audience: *Einstein on the Beach* was published in *Yale/Theatre*, Vol. 8, Nos. 2 & 3 (Spring, 1977).

"Nuclear Theatre" was published in the *Village Voice*, June 29, 1982.

I am grateful to Jadwiga Kosicka for specially translating from the Russian the letters of Anton Chekhov which appear in "Reading Chekhov."

Special thanks to Rosette Lamont who also advised me on the original Russian text of *Uncle Vanya*.

Photo credits: Leslie Cerier, 101 (left & center); Johan Elbers, 101 (right), 103 (bottom); Lois Greenfield, 94 (right), 95, 96; Nathaniel Tileston, 93, 94 (left), 100, 102, 103 (top), 104.

Library of Congress Cataloging in Publication Data
Theatrewritings
Library of Congress Catalog Card No.: 83-62618
ISBN: 0--933826-67-2 (cloth)
ISBN: 0-933826-68-0 (paper)

Printed in the United States of America

Publication of this book has been made possible in part by a grant from the National Endowment for the Arts, Washington, D.C., a federal agency, and public funds received from the New York State Council on the Arts.

THEATREWRITINGS

Contents

ENCOUNTERS

WRITERS II

Preface

IT USED TO BE A STANDARD JOKE THAT REPORTERS SHIFTED over from the sports pages of a newspaper when there was a vacancy at the drama desk. Following in that grand tradition I published my first pieces as the Sports Editor of my high school newspaper in the mid-sixties. Spectatorship is undifferentiated in the desire to be an audience. Perhaps the need comes to one early in life. In any case, I moved from the sports page to the arts page as an Editor on the college paper, and I was on my way. Why or even how I came to write about theatre, I don't know but the idea of theatre took over my life then, and continues to now. About thirteen years ago I began writing professionally in New York. My first pieces were articles, interviews and record reviews, everybody from Bessie Smith, Dory Previn, Cleo Laine to Scott Joplin, Frank Sinatra, Charles Aznavour. A feeling for music has always been important in my life, yet in the writing it came to take second place once I started graduate work in theatre. I only returned to writing about music again in 1983, to do the three music pieces which appear in this book. And yet, in some ways music is a greater passion than theatre.

Every few years or so when I have moved—New York forces you to do that—I would pack and unpack and then read old magazines and newspapers in which my early pieces had been published. As anyone who writes knows, re-reading one's writing can be like looking at old photographs. You see what you were, measure it against what you've become, and try to find some traces of the future you. But it also makes you look at yourself as if you were someone else because you lose the memory of yourself over the years. So it was when I read over my essays in order to organize *Theatrewritings*.

As I look back over those published here I read them as if I have come upon a lost diary, and yet at the same time I do not know how I wrote what I did. I'm not trying to be mystical because writing is hard work and that I can attest to, but what I mean is that at a certain point writing takes on a life of its own. It writes itself. When you try to save up ideas or certain phrases for future work, it snatches them away, incorporating these half thoughts in whatever writing is at hand (and I mean that literally because I write longhand, not on the typewriter). Sometimes you aren't even aware that you have been thinking about something so long until you re-read what you have written over the years. Writing lets you know when it wants to begin and when it is ready to stop. At that point, I begin to read my own writing as if it were the work of another writer. It leaves me and enters the world. It lives its own life among the things of the world.

No writing can be separated from the context of its time, and so I view my own writing as inseparably bound to the preceding fifteen or so years of theatre, what was significant, controversial, innovative then, how that reflected the larger movement of ideas and events that shaped contemporary experience. I am grateful that the beginning of my life as a writer coincided with the golden age of experiment in American theatre. I learned much from the artists who created this theatre, and what I have learned has helped me to understand my life outside of theatre. Theatre has become my way of life now. There is no more wonderful feeling for a young critic than to grow up alongside of an art form that is redefining itself, and making you throw away the conventional ideas you had only just learned.

Sometimes I had the feeling that I never wanted to write the last essay for this book—I would include something on Gertrude Stein, on Thornton Wilder, on Heiner Müller, on Witkiewicz, no I wouldn't—because I know it signifies a certain end for me, at the very least an end of the period of my life attached to a theatre that changed the way theatre is made all over the world. And yet I know sadly that the newness of this theatre, for something is new only once in a generation, is over too. Something is missing for me when I go to see a Mabou Mines or Richard Foreman production in a big budgeted, institutional space, with all its advertising needs. A dozen years ago I was one of only a handful of spectators seeing their work in a grungy loft or little theatre in a part of the city few people wandered into. Now I sit among people for whom this theatre has no urgency. Avant-garde theatre has moved into the culture machine but it still has no real impact in American cultural life and letters the way other arts do. All important theatre is dying from lack of attention in the discourse of American life, it has no input in the way we view our experience as a people. In fact, the whole feeling of going to the theatre and being part of the theatreworld has changed in the brief span of time this book covers: the difference is tied to aesthetic, cultural, social, and economic factors. Some of the pieces included here try to put the contemporary mood into perspective.

Theatrewritings is for me a personal journal in which my feelings about the world are tangled up with feelings about theatre and writing. Writing is the way I stage my thoughts. I don't know what I think about things unless I write about them. Now I feel emptied out because everything I think I know is in these pages. I have never believed that the essay is an "objective" form of writing. In many ways it is the most personal because it is so direct a statement of purpose.

The earliest essay in this book, "Peter Handke's *My Foot My Tutor*: Aspects of Modernism," was begun around 1973, initially planned for an M.A. thesis then abandoned, eventually published four years later in the *Michigan Quarterly Review*. The selections from *The Theatre of Images* were completed in 1975 though published two years later. The articles on Barbra Streisand, Judy Garland and music performance, "The Other Lillian Hellman" and "Reading Chekhov" were written especially for publication in *Theatrewritings*. Except for a few published elsewhere, most of the remaining pieces appeared in *Performing Arts Journal* between 1979-84. I have been the most fortunate of writers to have my own theatre journal, as blessed as any actor or director or playwright who has his or her own theatre. *Performing Arts Journal*, which I helped found in 1976 and have continued since to co-edit, urged me to be a writer by its very presence. I could write as long as I wanted, on any subject, in whatever shape. There is no greater luxury for a writer than a place to publish.

I would especially like to acknowledge the companionship of Gautam Dasgupta whose life I have shared for twelve years, and who has shared with me the making of Performing Arts Journal Publications. It was his intellectual brilliance that sparked my own life as a writer. I am also grateful to my good friend Rustom Bharucha for questioning with me the unfathomable process of writing. Together the three of us have often driven day into the night with our talk.

Bonnie Marranca

New York
March 1984

Writers I

Alphabetical Shepard
The Play of Words

the artist in spite of himself

In the relationship of artist and audience the private I devises strategies to evade the public eye. Like the jazz saxophonist Niles who commits suicide in B♭ —the "key" to the mysterious overture—Shepard wants to disappear into the text, and to leave behind for the critic/detective only his outline. Behind this emotional gesture is the radical ideal of the authorless work and the denial of the Author as Myth.

Bertolt Brecht and Sam Shepard

Brecht developed the concept of character as situated between the actor (I) and the role (you). Character created from the point of view of the third person (he), from outside the event: narrative acting. Shepard, a storyteller like Brecht, elaborates this idea by situating narration in the present, in the equation of character as narrator, and so eliminating *gestus* in favor of the tone of voice. He substitutes myth for history, experience for theory.

The Brechtian actor narrates from the outside in; it's the other way around—inside out—in Shepard. The Brechtian work sets each unit of the play against the larger background. Shepard, the hedonistic writer, enjoys every dramatic moment for its own sake. He writes as if there is no tomorrow.

character

1. What usually happens in the theatre is that the actor is given the opportunity to be a character. Shepard reverses the practice by giving his characters the chance to be performers.

2. Characters in his plays tell us about themselves rather than having other characters or the author tell us about them. They exist prior to the dramatic action, not because of it. When a character does not have to explain a play the play can tell itself: rather than being about something, it is the thing itself.

3. The "realistic" character is created by an actor who must develop an "inner life" for himself in order to play his character in full dimension. Shepard's principal characters already have an inner life. So, in effect, the character takes inner life from the province of the actor for his own. And, Shepard, understanding what it means to be an actor, incorporates what the actor prepares into his composition of character. The actor is then free to play the moment, not the whole play; free to express the quality of being rather than having been. The typical realistic character has to play the line of the dramatic text whereas in Shepard's radical transformation of realism the character plays fragments, gaps, transformations—the breaks in continuity.

4. Generally, character chases the illusory ideal of definition: if during the course of a play one keeps an account of the character's emotional and physical details, his center of self will be revealed. The Shepard character has not simply a self but several selves which are continually changing, closer in composition to the transformational character developed by The Open Theatre (the author's one time relationship with this group needs to be fully examined) than the typical dramatic character. The transformational character has a fluid relationship to changing "realities" whereas a character in realistic drama is fixed in his relationship to reality which is itself fixed.

the dramatic field

Conventional realism is a closed structure of scenes with a definable beginning, middle and end that proceeds in a straight line. Causality dominates the action and motivation the character: the outcome is predictable from the point of view of reason. It is a kind of structure that is only interested in the similarities of things.

Shepard's open realism exists in a dramatic field composed of events not scenes, of explosions and contradictions not causes, of the overall effect, of gestalts. It is characterized by disruption not continuity, by simultaneity not succession; it values anomalies not analogies. In other words, it captures a reality that disregards realism's supposition of the rational. It praises the differences, the irregularities between things, and can accommodate the simultaneity of experiences in expanded time/space. Consciousness as subject matter takes precedence over the machinations of plot. Based on an expressionist view of character, the dramatic field encourages the emotionalization of physical space through the outward expansion of personal, inner space. The text as dramatic field is the space of writing as the gesture of emotion.

Unfortunately, Shepard doesn't take advantage of his own sophisticated technique, preferring simple subject matter and plots, instead of complexly developed material. The scope of his dramatic fields does not live up to their potential as really demanding models of experience.

eat your heart out

1. How many of the plays can you name in which the characters do *not* eat or talk about food? Mostly, it's breakfast, the meal associated with the presence of the mother, the start of the new day, light after the darkness of night. Bacon and eggs. "Home" fries. Fresh coffee. Sometimes Rice Krispies. Speeches about food are often the most luxurious in the plays, yet Shepard is no gourmet and, in fact, has very simple tastes—he doesn't seem to care what he eats as long as he eats.

2. Eating is used as a way to evade emotion: sometimes it's a reaction to anxiety or fear, a response to traumatic external events. Let's not forget the pure pleasure of eating, its physical and spiritual nourishment, the suggestion of companionship. One associates it with a setting—a comfortable home or perhaps a chrome diner. Shepard is fetishistic about food which masks the real spiritual "hunger" only obliquely expressed. Brecht: "Grub first, then ethics."

3. Eating and making love: eating as sublimated sex. Is it any wonder that the speeches about food are so sensual, so seductive? Eating is about desire and fulfillment, as sex is.

the family that preys together stays together

1. *Curse of the Starving Class, Buried Child* and *True West* go beyond criticizing the moral and physical disintegration of the American family to an earnest investigation of what it means to be a member of a family. One of the more interesting aspects of these plays is, unlike the typical American family play written since the war, they seem more able to integrate highly individualistic, even eccentric behavior, and so are more in tune with the kinds of comedies written

in the twenties and thirties than those of today. (Interestingly, California playwrights are now outlining this notion.)

2. The sons are the only normative figures in these domestic dramas. The parents are shown to be comic-pathetic, dreamy figures unable to comprehend or initiate events. They are failures as parent figures, and more troubled and out of control than their children.

3. All three of the plays are structured more around dialogue than the solo (in *Curse* and *Buried Child* the son and grandson/son have one solo each, but there are none in *True West*) which signals an emphatic shift in the pattern of discourse—away from characters who are obsessive and self-absorbed, and toward the development of relationships between characters. In the earlier two plays one could hardly conceive of the dialogue as a "conversational flow" but conversation does flow in *True West* which is perhaps the most conventional play Shepard has ever written.

The fact that dialogue is becoming a strong, integrated force in the plays indicates a new strain in Shepard's work, a shift in subject matter from displacement to roots, and an interest in the continuity of relationships rather than their disintegration, and finally, an emotional broadening of character.

geographies of the spirit

1. In *Angel City* the West is described as the "Looks-Within" place "for looking inside yourself," while the East is "the place of illumination." And, in *Rolling Thunder Logbook* Shepard writes,

> . . . Jesse James, Billy the Kid, Mickey Free, Buffalo Bill. Tales grew around them mostly out of a giant communications gap between the solid intellectual East Coast and the wide-open mysteries of the West.

Further along in the book he asks, "Is Boston all that heavy as the papers make out?" Shepard values the mythical status of places, as if to reinforce William Gass's contention that the only history America can have is a geographic one.

Cody (*Geography of a Horse Dreamer*) can't dream up winning horses because he doesn't know which part of the country he's in; Jeep (*Action*) is having an emotional crisis because he's lost his sense of place.

The axis of this poetics of space is not only East/West. In *Icarus's Mother* the opposition is North/South when the unknown pilot writing in the sky unwittingly creates for the picnickers beneath him a language of the apocalypse:

$E = mc^2$. Salvation lay in the direction of the mountains in *Operation Side-winder*, in the desert in *True West*.

2. The landscape of the body: the shape the character creates when his imagination transforms his body (Kent in *La Turista*); the outline of an identity that wants to hide in anonymity (Niles in *Suicide in B♭*); a character describing what it feels like inside his body (Stu in *Chicago*). In Shepard's non-psychological drama, the bodies do the thinking.

At times the body strains toward the fourth dimension. One of the key points in the plays is that of the soul or "I" as an entity separate from the physical body. Shepard's characters want out-of-the-body experiences. Often the characters seem able to observe themselves from the outside; some want to be free of their bodies, or break through to another level of reality; and still others lament their bodies' rhythm as slower than their mental states.

3. Shepard's most moving portrait of the American experience, *Action*, was written while he was living in England. The distance was not only geographic but emotional, intellectual, political, historical. Curiously, this is the only play, by Shepard's own admission, he had ever read aloud to himself, as if the sound of the voice could echo across the Atlantic as some aural image of the distressed voice of America. In England he would, as a character, live the feeling of displacement and loss of community of the characters in his play. He would know what it means to be surrounded by people who speak a language different from his own, for surely British English is not American English. By reading the play aloud he tells himself a story—in a lean, affective tone—that is his own story. The triumph of *Action* is that it defines Nixonian America in a jagged, constrained structure that mirrors the very difficulty of finding a language of social communication and a means to express feeling: on a very basic level, *Action* is about the loss of language. The vision of Walt Whitman's America is brutally contrasted with what America had become. And like Whitman, Shepard, in his finest play, was able to link his personal experience to the national experience. *Action* is political in the most subtle sense—because his political feelings have more to do with people than systems Shepard uses metaphors instead of direct address to express himself—and yet it is one of the few American plays of its time to capture the cultural moment with any degree of intensity.

4. Shepard's magnificent obsession is the loss of individualism through control by unnameable, outside forces which is really fear of the loss of personal space. The prolonged reverie of the lyrical voice is an extension of the character's emotional space, his mapping of consciousness; it is also the defense mechanism of the individual that keeps "society" from impinging upon the ter-

ritory of the imagination.

5. Most of American drama is claustrophobic: it takes place in a cluttered living room, dining room, or kitchen. If you think of plays that are "spacious" only a few examples come to mind, these writers in particular: Thornton Wilder, a mid-Westerner whose great achievement, *Our Town*, defied conventional time and space and made the sense of place a philosophical concern and subject matter. And Gertrude Stein who based many of her ideas about drama on the plays she saw in San Francisco—who but a Californian (even if she lived there briefly) could conceive of a play as a "landscape"? Neither of them was interested in psychology (as Shepard himself is not) which can only contain the spirit, make it definable, regulate its situation in time and space.

Shepard's work should be viewed in this context of a larger, non-urban scale. His feeling of space (and nature) is of a vastness that seems unfathomable, generous, still, triumphant, even religious (his transcendental heritage)—simply there. Space that draws consciousness in on itself because next to it the physical scale of the individual is trivial; a space that looks from the Pacific clear across America, and across deserts, unflinching in their refusal to adapt to changing times. In this world people can afford to be talkers and dreamers because the space they inhabit is lyrical. Only Southerners and Westerners, people who understand attachment to the land, retain the gift of gab and the tall tale, even the art of conversation; we in the Northeast have lost it to the urban language of the concrete phrase. Shepard is the only American dramatist writing today to evoke a new sense of space in drama, and he transfers the values of the American West and its ideals into the emotional landscapes of his plays, highlighting the function of *space as myth*. This is where the discussion of regionalism in drama can begin.

the horizontal and the vertical

The solo is vertical: it finds an image to start with and soars through layer upon layer of physical and emotional detail. However, only the male voice moves on this vertical, rhythmic trajectory. The women in the plays rarely have these personal solos, though *Red Cross* is an exception, and even so it doesn't detail a uniquely female experience of the world. Female discourse is horizontal, circumscribed by its orientation toward the others in the play: harmonic.

the rhythm of imagery

1. The solo carries Charles Olson's idea of "projective verse" into drama: ONE PERCEPTION MUST IMMEDIATELY LEAD TO A FURTHER PERCEP-TION. Olson equated speech (the poet's) with performance but he didn't

follow the implications of his own manifesto far enough into theatre where it finds a logical application: here the author's breath span is actually translated to the performer as a voice in the theatrical experience. Perversely, one can say that theatre aestheticizes the notion of artificial respiration.

What Shepard does in his best work is to open up the emotional terrain of a character so he can project his feelings OUT THERE. The emotions of the character are the projections of his personal imagery, beginning usually with a single perception and building into a long string of images (verbal, visual, aural) that embroider the initial perception or image beyond the immediate situation of the character to an area of his imagination.

2. Shepard's frequent difficulty in ending his plays (for examples, *La Turista*, *Angel City*, *Curse of the Starving Class*) is directly related to the explosion of images that accumulate in strength and autonomy throughout each play. He seems to run away from the energy he unleashes in his characters, unable to confront and control the rhythms of imagery he himself has set in motion.

3. Imagery vs. symbol: imagery is dynamic ("meaning" is not fixed), non-psychological because it is not tied to motivation; theatrical because it outlines its own space. The symbol is static (it generally has the same repertoire of meaning wherever it appears), psychological because it reflects literal states of mind; literary because it speaks a familiar language. (For example, the airplane in *Icarus's Mother* is imagery whereas the vegetables in the garden in *Buried Child* are symbolic.) The symbol is a fairly literal transposition of a certain thematic aspect of a play; representational in attitude it simply reinforces what is already there. Imagery is metaphoric, it has more possibilities, it is presentational; it functions simultaneously on several different levels. Imagery subsumes symbols in a larger meaning. To the extent that Shepard's plays remain in the realm of the trope they highlight their feeling for imagery. Plays such as *Seduced*, *Buried Child* and *True West* are less provocative than Shepard's metaphoric work because their symbolic language is familiar.

4. In its most destructive frame the image can lead to aestheticized feeling—the absence of real feeling—or the substitution of a picture of something for the real thing. If American culture is moving more and more toward the production and consumption of imagery, it has to do with the aestheticizing of feeling, of history, of the self, of politics, of personal relations; our fragmented world has lost the means to express itself in a unified symbology. The contemporary way of expressing the world and the self is through imagery. The symbol reflects a wholeness, a shared system of values and experience that is largely absent from contemporary life which is dominated by the images of things, not the things themselves. Shepard's use of realism as a form reflects the preponderance of im-

ages as opposed to symbols which as a unifying element have always dominated realism in its most traditional examples.

jazz

Shepard prefaces *Angel City* with this "Note to the Actors":

> Instead of the idea of a "whole character" with logical motives behind his behavior which the actor submerges himself into, he should consider himself a fractured whole with bits and pieces of character flying off the central theme. In other words, more in terms of collage construction or jazz improvisation.

Characterization in the play follows the structural make-up of improvisation to the point of building into a musical finale of Act I that has the actors (or are they performers?) jamming. The appeal of jazz is more than structural. As an approach to composition it embodies an attitude that is at the heart of Shepard's work: spontaneity of expression. Not chance, but improvisation.

Angel City is Shepard's big jazz ensemble piece; elsewhere jazz is reflected in the free association of long solos (particularly in the early plays) which seem to make themselves up as they go along. They follow the same principle as jazz improvisation—composition by digression. For Shepard it means being able to go with the flow of words, as his literary big brother Jack Kerouac described it, in more sensual terms, writing whatever "comes into your head as it comes."

The jazz artist teases the audience into following his rhythm for as long as he can keep it going, lifting them to a tantalizing high, taking them down, bringing them up again, one tempo to another, a little bit at a time as if they were caught in a sexual embrace with music that continually forestalls the orgasmic response of applause and shouts. The most powerful solo parts in Shepard's plays have that same erotic effect which is what makes his writing sexy though there's no actual sex in it: it's the rhythm of sex not the representation of it. Shepard's seduction is linguistic—a coming to language then to speech.

kitsch as myth

Vintage Chevys, old Packards, chrome diners, and Hudson Hornets are objects turned subjects in a nostalgia for pop artifacts. Kitsch as romanticized attachment to the mass-culture object, turning common imagery into art. ("Romanticism is the mother of kitsch": Hermann Broch.) In a society which easily discards old products and artifacts in a frantic race to produce new ones, the discarded object as setting quickly attains special status. The outmoded consumer object—in its nostalgic setting—is America's historical ruin.

"land of the free"

The spirit of the American West, its triumph of individualism, unlimited potential, transcendant beauty, and disdain of regulation is the soul of Shepard's
work. It is also the same philosophy that put Ronald Reagan in the White
House. There is nothing wrong with loving your country, which Shepard
does—and Reagan does, too—but the frontier ethic turns ugly when set in
global, even national perspective.

What's problematic in Shepard's thinking is his overly Romantic, self-satisfied
view of the historical past (even as a presence in the plays) and his inability to
examine the implications of this position in broad terms.

Side by side with Shepard's glorification of the frontier ethic, and its con-
comitant isolationism, oppressive view of women, retreat from group concerns,
is his sixties-style radical politics with its dread of the "system," its pastoral
ideals, and persistent criticism of the American way of life. There's always been
this tug-of-war between radical ideals—however more emotionally felt than
politically reasoned—and a deeply-felt conservatism that is never fully resolved
in the plays and, in fact, is the source of their political tension. This duality
which, sadly, history has shown resolves itself to the right, embodies all that is
good and bad in the conscience of the American people, it is its promise and
failure, and, more significantly, the basis of its doctrine of rebirth. It is the mark
of Shepard's provincialism and his essential Americanness.

the melodramatic imagination

1. The Shepard mystique is grounded in the image of a cool, laid back cowboy,
an outsider, a man in control of things. Yet, if you look at the plays they suggest an author given to hysteria, even paranoia, an author who views life
melodramatically by magnifying an ordinary event until it attains the proportions of a disaster. What's true in part is made to define the whole perspective.
The figurative devices of metaphor and metonymy that dominate Shepard's
writing are easily linked to melodrama: they make what is absent from a text
seem more important than what is present in it.

2. Shepard the moralist. Melodrama equals a drama of oppositions: hero vs.
villain, individual vs. system, intellect vs. emotion, artist vs. public, East vs.
West, inside vs. outside. Shepard's plays are always communicating the loss,
and the corruption of ideals, without offering solutions and without actually
dealing with moral issues. His morality is hidden in form.

3. Melodrama and American drama. Unlike European drama in which irony and cynicism have dominated since the modern period, American drama is predominantly melodrama—it is idealistic, moralistic, emotional, it simplifies issues. Characters generally say what they mean, believing in language as means of communication. If the response to the void for most of modern drama is silence, for Shepard's characters it is talking as a way of coping with emotional stress. His characters have not lost faith in the promise of a return to innocence, they still mourn their fall from grace. Nietzsche: "I fear we are not getting rid of God because we still believe in grammar." American drama refuses to believe the European position: that God is dead.

narration

1. By American standards of dramaturgy the speeches of Shepard's characters are too long and too narrative. Much of the background of the plays is narrated; events which don't occur on stage are narrated; narration is used as a purely informational device; the solo itself breaks apart the structure by reconstituting the narrative line as a rejection of dialogue and an act of imagination. The movement of the plays, in general, subverts discourse, character, dramatic action, and setting, all of the elements by which the "puzzle" of a play is traditionally fitted together. The plays are always coming apart at the seams because they are constructed out of pieces, and even so, many of the plays refuse to end. The plays mitigate against the ideal of conceiving work as a totality, on a unified scale, offering instead only a sampling of feelings and events that have to be experienced in segments. The structure of the narratives reflects the way Americans experience everyday life—in fits and spurts, and surface impressions, suffering the loss of extended conversation as a way of communicating feeling. Through his revitalization of realism Shepard has been able remarkably to show changes in the structure of experience in America. His plays change the contours of speech and, therefore, communication in realism.

2. The breakdown of dialogue. Reliance on narration instigates the devaluation of dialogue. The plays can hardly be said to have a conversational flow when characters are often unaware of what each other is saying, or they ignore it, and rarely do they comment on what has been said. Extended dialogue is occasional, as if conversation were pre-empted by the other languages of the stage, imagery for one.

Conversational dialogue has come increasingly to be disvalued in American theatre, almost exclusively by avant-garde groups from The Living Theatre to the present whose work has reflected new psychoanalytic theories and a general drift toward narrative, presentational modes of acting rather than motivational, representational acting. Before writer-directors such as Richard Foreman, Robert Wilson and Lee Breuer were writing texts that broke down the structure of dialogue and elevated the solo voice—taking consciousness as subject matter—Shepard had already moved in this direction in his early plays. Of *American* playwrights, only Gertrude Stein had preceded him.

The disavowal of dialogue as the prime mover of the dramatic line suggests a drama that is not exclusively rooted in the manifestation of conflict between characters, but one that is more internalized in the self. (For example, much of the drama written today by women is simply the stringing together of monologues, as if there is first the need to tell all about oneself rather than a story; on the other hand, black drama has always been based on dialogue, conflict between characters, and behavior rooted in relationships.) Spalding Gray's solo, autobiographical talking pieces—pure narrative—in which he constructs his personal history for an audience, is the evolutionary end product of the breakdown of dialogue in theatre.

3. The current rejection of dialogue, and Shepard's plays up to his most recent few reflect this, signals a presentation of character that owes less to Freudian psychology than to the development of the narcissistic personality which is increasingly defining the individual of today—in cultural, sociological and psychological terms. The implications of this change are undeniable: the breakdown of dialogue reflects in its dramatic form the overly analytical exploration of the self and the inability to sustain relationships that characterize behavior today. To the extent that they emphasize individuals in their world, Shepard's characters illustrate the contemporary malaise. To the extent that they refuse to give up the uniqueness of the individual imagination to group psychology they are a mode of survival in an institutionalized world.

ontology of the sentence

How the rhythm of speech evolves from the emotional line of the moment:

When Wesley describes the drunken return of his father (*Curse of the Starving Class*) he begins in a leisurely, joyous, personal mood ("I could feel myself in my bed in my room in this house in this town in this state in this country") then moves to a quick rush of incomplete sentences. Images are set in short phrases whose staccato rhythm echoes his heart beating ("Man throwing wood. Man throwing up. Mom calling cops. Dad crashing away. Back down driveway. Car door slamming. Ignition grinding. Wheels screaming"). The dangling participle used to recall the past event pushes it along as if it were happening now.

Howard's imagination takes flight like the plane overhead (*Icarus's Mother*); he needs conjunctions to do it:

> Lake after lake with river after river running away from the lake and going to the ocean. House after house turning into city after city and town after town.

His topographical essay is narrated from the point of view of the pilot.

The style match of *The Tooth of Crime*, one of the author's many plays about the artist and his relation to society, calls for poetry: Hoss's rhythm and blues truth ("You lost the barrelhouse you lost the honkey-tonk") vying with Crow's superficial punchline ("Talkin' sock it to it, get the image in line"). This talking rock piece has a syntax like good guitar licks—all rhythm and no harmony.

In the meta-language world of *Tooth*, two different (musical) languages confront each other in a fusillade of metaphors. *Tooth* is about making up language and using it to manipulate reality. Hoss eventually commits suicide because he can't adopt Crow's "language" (verbal or gestural)—in Shepard's conception of character speech is so integrated with individual being that for any character to imitate someone else and transform his way of speaking (that is, his way of thinking) is to give up his identity.

In "Rhythm" (*Hawk Moon*) the more than page long catalogue of images is all percussion, run-on incomplete sentences isolating a single aural or visual rhythm.

> Dog claws clicking on hardwood floors. Clocks. Piston rhythms. Dripping faucets. Tin hitting tin in the wind. Water slapping rocks. Flesh slapping flesh. Boxing rhythms. Racing rhythms. Rushing brooks. . . .

play/pretend/performance

1. The Pirandellian character wears a mask which allows him to reflect the philosophical viewpoint of the playwright, formalized in the "play-within-the-play" structure. Shepard's characters, having been influenced by both Pirandellian theatricalism and the narrative acting of the Brechtian character, though not Genet's social perspective, is free to remove his mask. He knows he is a performer, and takes the opportunity whenever he wants to, to leave, mentally and in another time frame, the play and verbalize or act out his emotional responses to events around him. There is no such thing as illusion vs. reality, only shifting realities. In Shepard's work there is not the play-within-the-play, but *play within the play*. His plays are written from the point of view of the actor, and so incorporate the notion of performance.

2. Instead of thinking of the character as an actor who is playing a role, it seems more appropriate in the case of Shepard to think of the character as a performer—not acting a role, but improvising, in public, aspects of his private, imaginative life. Pirandello's characters were conceived at a time when the individual was believed to have both a public side and a private side. Since then, however, cultural, social and technological forces have conspired to eclipse the individual's private side; in effect, the public side has emerged, in the last twenty years, to be the measure of the individual.

The contemporary individual is less interested in playing several roles than in conceptualizing (creating images of) a whole new self: it's today's recycled notion of what was formerly called "upward mobility." In role-playing the situation sets the scene, but in "performance" the individual sets up the situation. (Sociologist Erving Goffman's theories seem irrelevant vis-à-vis Shepard. Goffman, who is interested in defining the self in relation to social roles, regards performance as an attitude toward *communication*. Shepard's characters do not relate to society, there is no world outside, they often cannot see beyond their own mental states. They react, they do not interact.)

3. Since the sixties the culture has tended increasingly to define all aspects of human interaction—politics, law, business, psychoanalysis, sexuality, work—in terms of performance (the term used to mean "behavior" or "accomplishment" unless, of course, one was speaking of the theatre). Now, life is viewed in terms of spectacle. The very make-up of Shepard's characters reflects the author's belief in performance—that is, the spontaneous creation of other scenarios within the main storyline of the play—as a technique for dealing with the "reality" of a given moment. His characters make spectacles of themselves.

In a country where the non-fatalistic, fluid concept of self supercedes class, professional and ideological formalities, the notion of human potential—the potential for changing into someone else (making yourself up)—predominates. The great irony in all of this is that an actor is now president, politics having united with entertainment as the current great performance opportunities. In an America that has become more and more self-conscious of its forms, and the parody of them, performance style is all.

4. There are no "performances" in *Operation Sidewinder, Curse of the Starving Class, Buried Child* and *True West* because the characters are caught up in the world of Fate, Necessity. Performance is an ironic attitude, not a tragic one.

quotations without quotation marks

Everybody's got a language. Shepard writes American regional speech, contemporary slang, cowboy dialect; the jargon of sports, car racing, gangsters; the doublespeak of disk jockeys, high tech and science fiction; the platitudes of Republican America, quasi-militants and Hollywood; the talking music of old bluesmen, young punks and rock and rollers.

Quotation is a natural critique of language but it rarely functions in the plays philosophically (cf. Peter Handke's *Sprechstücke*) or politically (cf. Heathcote Williams's *AC/DC*). Because he is more interested in talking than language per se, Shepard focuses on the idea of *speech as myth*. Quotation in its American usage (Ronald Tavel, Lee Breuer, Robert Wilson) is more poetic than political in its orientation because the American voice is classless.

varieties of religious experience

Christian symbolism and the development of Christian themes is an aspect of the plays that profoundly describes the context of Shepard's output. Corruption and its physical manifestation organizes the symbolism of *Angel City*'s slimy green ooze and the power-grabbing hands of Hackamore in *Seduced*. The return of the prodigal son Vince in *Buried Child* is also a fairly obvious interpretation of character. With great brio Weston, the buffoonish father in *Curse of the Starving Class*, is born again after being baptized in his own dirty bath water.

While these plays easily allude to Christian themes, *Operation Sidewinder* develops an elaborate repertoire of symbols out of the contradictory sources of the Bible, technological manuals and Indian ritual to demonstrate the Origin and the Fall, as dramatized by American life. The snake/computer in the desert/Eden is the dominant image in the play, doubling as a symbolism of evil that is transvalued into an Indian spirit of salvation.

Even more poignantly The Young Man, whose lost soul is eventually redeemed, is cleansed of Original Sin—loss of his spiritual values—in a baptism of fire at the apocalypse. His symbolic reenactment of confession is individualized in a language dominated by traditional symbols of evil:

> I devour the planet . . . I came to infect the continent . . . To spread my disease . . . To cut down the trees, to dig out the gold, to shoot down the deer, to capture the wind . . .

Shepard's plays are acts of faith, and his emotional response to being an American reflects the characteristic American pursuit of rebirth, and its opposite, the denial of history.

Gertrude Stein and the American experience

G.S.: "The business of art is to live in the actual present, that is the complete actual present, and to express that complete actual present."

Stein and Shepard seem at first an unlikely pair but they are quintessential American writers who have understood at once the American preference for the spontaneous and experiential grasp of a phenomenon. Both are obsessed with examining the immediacy of the present, and in minute detail. Description becomes a function of consciousness, a way to convey the fullness and fluidity of the moment; only then can the event of the past be present in the memory of the one speaking. Language creates reality. The personal experience of time is valued over conventional dramatic time, and personal expression is valued over the etiquette of narrative form. Shepard's characters corroborate the continuing truth of Stein's observation that "sentences are not emotional, and paragraphs are." It's the only way obsessive talkers can communicate.

Stein and Shepard: They've produced narcissistic characters who will tell you more than you want to know about them.

talking/telling stories

1. Characters who talk are different from characters who speak. In plays dominated by dialogue characters speak lines, and when the solo dominates a character can be said to talk. Talking comes from the performer (I) whereas speaking comes from the role player (he).

2. The virtuosic soloists in the plays are great talkers. The solo (performative) as opposed to the monologue (literary) stands apart from the action around or behind it and creates a life of its own, for as long as it desires. The soloist inhabits a different space temporarily; an inner, emotional space that others cannot enter because it is a personal space. It's the talking out of feelings that dominates the characters' lives, very rarely the direct expression of emotion in relation to another person.

3. Much of the solos consists of story-telling bits. Little stories, self-contained—they're about the speaker or an event he makes up or describes, not the story of the play itself. Shepard's characters are accomplished storytellers because they'd rather talk than act. Since their colleagues on stage are rarely listening to them they speak for themselves and for the audience. What Shepard has done is to link the oral tradition of poetry to the dramatic tradition, erasing the difference (momentarily) between drama (literature) and theatre (literature performed).

4. The Romantic poet thinks in the breathtaking/breathgiving line of poetry. The rhapsodic solo is the "song of myself" that was sung by the first beat poet, Walt Whitman, then by Kerouac and Ginsburg, and now by Shepard's characters, who carry the beat legacy into dramatic form.

urban cowboy

1. The contemporary counterpart of the cowboy is the rock star, also a man who stands outside the system—the would-be rock-and-roll Jesus with a cowboy mouth. The metaphoric translation of the cowboy showdown appears in *Tooth of Crime* when two rock stars compete for territory and status in a style match that spits words instead of bullets; the groupie Becky is a contemporary version of the gun moll. *Tooth of Crime* exorcises the spirit of cowboy mouth—in real rock terms, look what the new rock star, Crow, promises for the future.

2. Cowboys, too. The image of the cowboy helps Shepard bring the ideal of play into adult life, it establishes a continuity of imagination. The cowboy represents a longing after heroes and heroic deeds which is often at the center of Shepard's plays, and is the heart of American West mythology. Even Henry Kissinger couldn't resist comparing himself to a cowboy: "This amazing, romantic character suits me precisely because to be alone has always been part of my style or, if you like, my technique."

voices

How to read Shepard: don't look at the name of the character—you will know who is talking from the rhythm and tone of his voice.

Individualism finds its truest manifestation in the way each character uniquely shapes language. It is always the character you hear, not the author, and as many characters as he creates there are distinct speech patterns.

Shepard's characters love to hear themselves talk, they may even repeat a line of dialogue or a cliché or phrase in a few different ways, as if a voice talking, or imagining out loud, could, if only momentarily, control or create reality.

the zero gravity of women

1. One of the most problematic aspects of the plays is Shepard's consistent refusal or inability, whichever the case may be, to create female characters whose imaginative range matches that of the males. Women are the background of the plays: they hang out and make themselves useful for chores

while the men make the decisions, take risks, face challenges, experience existential crises. Women are frequently abused, and always treated as subservient to men, their potential for growth and change restricted.

For a young man Shepard's portrayal of women is as outdated as the frontier ethic he celebrates: men have their showdowns or face the proverbial abyss while the women are absorbed in simple activities and simplistic thoughts. They are wives, girlfriends, mothers or some sort of servile worker (maid, secretary); in other words, always connected to someone or something, never simply women whose consciousness might be revealed with the degree of intensity a man's is. There is no expression of a female point of view in any of Shepard's plays. Even the stage directions can be used to indicate a woman's lack of individuation (Honey in *Operation Sidewinder*), and some women are interchangeable (Mom in *True West* is just the leftover Halie from *Buried Child*).

The heroism and strength of the cowboy is revered by Shepard but in actuality the men he creates are ineffectual, fearful, and emotionally immature. They show no strength or character or will, yet they are allowed to dominate because it is their due as men.

2. Shepard has no apparent interest in the relations of men and women, preferring instead to write about male experience. He writes as if he is unaware of what has been happening between men and women in the last decade. Though he has opened up whole new areas of exploration in the form of dramatic realism developed by his literary forefathers, he has not radicalized the way women interact in dramatic form, neither has he given them a new language, and, in fact, his female characters are much less independent and intelligent that many of those created by these forefathers a hundred years ago.

It cannot be ignored that Shepard, who is in some ways an idol of his young audiences, is not simply traditional in his view of women, but downright oppressive. One of the reasons why the lyrical solo is not characteristic of female expression is that the women are rarely given anything to say that can stand alone. The voice—of consciousness, of the emotions, of reason, of triumph, and of failure, too—and finally, of America—is a man's voice.

3. The only truly dominant, autonomous female character in the plays is Cavale in *Cowboy Mouth*, and it took a Patti Smith, ironically an artist who had molded herself in the Romantic tradition of the male artist/outlaw, to write her part for herself. The one character written by Shepard who comes close to rebelling aginst female stereotypes is Emma in *Curse of the Starving Class* but she is written as a tomboy—a tough high school kid who tears up a local bar, and plans to work her way to Mexico hauling in barracuda, fixing four-

wheel drives, learning how to be a short order cook while writing novels on the side. Something along the lines of a Jack Kerouac. Rebellion and individuality are given a specifically male character. When Emma's own female "curse" is linked poetically to the fall of her class, it makes one ask if Shepard isn't cursing women for their powers of reproduction.

4. Shepard conceives of space—emotional, intellectual, physical—as a male domain, a territorial imperative, as it were. The landscape of the female body has yet to appear, but when a language of the sexes and female language are added to all the other "languages" he has mastered, the silent voices in the plays will tell their stories.

X: *known and unknown*

The object of closed, conventional dramaturgy: to make known every factor. It operates on the principle of subtraction: environment minus character minus gesture equals meaning. The open text as dramatic field multiplies each of its autonomous elements to generate unforeseeable sets of possibilities as its algebra of emotion.

"You act yourself out"

In *Action*—a play that centers on the experience of entropy—the isolated characters view themselves from the outside. Jeep: "I can even imagine how horrifying it could be to be doing all this, and it doesn't touch me. It's like I'm dismissed." Shooter literally acts himself out (as a dancing bear, a turtle, as a father in a comfortable chair): these moments of acting out function for him as a survival mechanism. They are the only emotional responses he is capable of.

The flip side of keeping in control is getting caught in the image of yourself which you are acting out. "I made myself up," Henry Hackamore boasts, having been seduced by the images of power he himself has fabricated. "I was taken by the dream and all the time I thought I was taking it."

Kent acts himself right out of his body and out of *La Turista*'s plot as he creates a Frankenstein fantasy, an existential horror scenario in which man and beast engage in the ultimate confrontation.

(If performance is an ironic and comic attitude toward the self, acting yourself out is its existential, tragic opposite.)

2. The endings of the plays mentioned above are essentially the same: Jeep, Henry and Kent confront their terror of losing control by attempting to tran-

scend physical space—Jeep by moving around the stage as if "he's attempting his own escape from the space he's playing in," Henry by pretending he's flying, Kent by lunging through the upstage wall of the set. These plays have to end because the major characters have left metaphorically, even literally, the space the other characters inhabit. When all else fails you act yourself out. For Shepard space is more than setting—it develops its own thematics rather than remaining decorative, functional or symbolic.

3. One of the most interesting usages of this mode of behavior is in *Tooth of Crime* in a dialogue Hoss, about to meet his challenger, Crow, devises. The voice of "Yer old Dad" intrudes to offer some reassuring words to a frightened son. In therapeutic terms, the acting out helps Hoss objectify and get a grasp on the situation.

the zone of myth

The theatre experience exists in the space between what is there in the performing space and what is not there. The power of Shepard's plays is in what is absent from the event, that space he leaves for the spectator's imagination to play in. The Shepard play is a metaphoric model of the American experience, localized in fictional characters. The empty space in the contemporary mind is the space from which myth has absented itself: Shepard tries to fill that space. And by being so generous with his feelings, another myth is outlined—that of the artist, in spite of himself.

[1981]

The Self as Text
Lee Breuer's *Animations*

LOOKING OVER SOME NOTES I HAD MADE HALF A DOZEN YEARS ago after an early viewing of *The Red Horse Animation* I found this scribbling: "emotions are entirely formal." I didn't realize the implications of the remark at the time but after a few more years of seeing Mabou Mines perform the animations (*Red Horse, B.Beaver, Shaggy Dog*) written for them by Lee Breuer in the period 1968-78, and reading the texts themselves, my initial comment seemed comprehensible in the context of the deeper structures of the trilogy. The texts began to make sense as Breuer's formalization of his own emotions.

It has always seemed disconcerting that the achievement of the animations as one of the major works of the American theatre in the seventies was based on the productions alone. As if the writing had no identity of its own apart from the productions. Breuer's direction of the animations, it is true, gave primacy to production values, and to some extent that choice has denied him his due as a writer.

In my Introduction to the comic book version of *Red Horse* published in *The Theatre of Images* I emphasized the work's performance aspects because it was my intention then to develop a performance vocabulary, not a poetics of narrative. Now I find it more compelling to look at the animations from a literary point of view, and to put aside temporarily Breuer's directorial conceptions to deal with him as a writer—to be more specific, to consider him as a playwright. The texts have a life of their own apart from their presentation in performance, and they can be read and enjoyed as literature—as plays. It is not my intention now to search for "a meaning" in each animation but to uncover the multiplicity of meanings each work contains. In other words, to approach each animation in a way that embraces its unique sensuality in an equitable union of form and content: to highlight its structures of feeling. To the extent that the animations function on an autobiographical level, the area I want to focus on in this essay, Breuer-as-writer reveals his personal relationship to his art, and his feelings about being an artist.

Many artists draw all their resources from themselves and continually reflect only their own image. Breuer's use of autobiography, however, goes way beyond a purely narcissistic approach; he is self-projected, not self-centered. By that I mean he situates himself in a social context, and what he writes in his plays relates to the world around him. It is the I in "the world," not the "I" in its own world. If the animations can be said to treat consciousness from three different perspectives, and I believe that they can, what Breuer develops throughout them is a highly skillful thematics of consciousness.

He does this not through the projection of an omnipotent "I" but through the personalities of animals who, instead of people, are the principal "characters" in the plays. The notion of "animation" refers to the life spirit (the soul) he gives them. (Here it might be worth considering Roland Barthes's distinction beween "figuration" and "representation" of the author in the text, the former based on presence, the latter on description.) Drawing on the rich and popular historical tradition of the beast epic Breuer creates his own fables of contemporary life and manners, telling us in his own punning fashion how the individual functions as a social "animal." These fables operate on at least two levels: metaphorically, they function as art about making art; mythically, they work to demystify stereotypical attitudes about malehood.

Breuer's choice of animals is not arbitrary, but works as a kind of totemic classification. The natural activities of each animal's (horse, beaver, dog) life are made to coincide with human modes of feeling and perception in the context of the plays. In this way, the horse evokes feelings of freedom and romance, the beaver creates defenses, and the dog is caught in a master/slave relationship. All of the latter are metaphors for certain intellectual and emotional positions, and are played with on several levels. And at the same time, from the mythic perspective Breuer debunks the male prerogative of knowing who you are. The metaphoric and mythic fuse and interact contrapuntally in the narrative line of the texts, with the metaphoric inviting a partly psychoanalytic approach, and the mythic the more structural.

By using metaphors of animals instead of an identifiable self Breuer distances himself from his material, allowing him to take an ironic stance toward it which he does every chance he gets. The result is literally a cross between the irony of Kafka's fables and the hyperbole of the animated cartoon, by Breuer's own admission the two most influential sources of the animation concept. The literary conceit of the fable gives him complete freedom of expression while at the same time offering the protection of a mask. Breuer has devised his texts in such a way that they show the "eye" looking at the "I." It is from this perspective that the animations reveal, not facts of life, but aspects of existence.

The use of autobiography, in the sense of the "self as text," is one of the characteristic features of current experimental theatre and performance art which in the seventies has been evolving new strategies for dealing with content. If theatre in the sixties was defined by the collaborative creation of the text, in recent years individual authorship has gained ascendancy; likewise, theatre in the sixties (and all offshoots of the Happenings, too) was outer-directed whereas now it (and performance art) is inner-directed: perhaps the shift can be said to be from the exploration of environmental space to the exploration of mental space, and from narration to documentation. Following the current interest in America in a highly refined spiritual life and the evolution of new shapes of consciousness, the performing arts are actively redefining their own spirit. In both cases, the emphasis is on the dialogue with the self.

The animations, in particular, show a conscious development of personal mythology, a tendency to be found in the plays of Richard Foreman and Spalding Gray, and the operas of Meredith Monk, just to name a few examples. It seems more than coincidental that both Breuer and Gray refer to their work under the title of "trilogy" and that Foreman has evolved a "cycle" of plays with the same themes and characters. In my view this terminology reflects the authors' decided attempts to develop continuing self-histories—a fact which is not surprising because Americans have always defined themselves as individuals, not as a society or group.

In a larger context Breuer seems to be following the mythopoeic strain in the American avant-garde (some examples: The Living Theatre, The Open Theater, Robert Wilson); for the seventies I think we can redefine this strain as "auto-mythopoeic." The Romantic self is very much evident in Breuer's animations and Breuer, whose oeuvre is based on the life of the spirit, is the most expressionistic, poetic (and literary) of his contemporaries. The animations are Breuer's memory of the past (documentary time) related in the present (narrative time), the temporal narrative lines fusing in a self-conscious consciousness. *Animations* continues the American tradition of transcendentalism.

Breuer animates his work with his own life spirit, the deepest part of his being. The part Charles Olson called the poet's "breath." It is this breath which gives life to the animals, and "animates" them so that they "become" human. Then Breuer's literary imagination takes over, letting all his feelings and perceptions loose in an idiosyncratic stream of consciousness that reflects a funky speechifying animal double. In this universe of words that each animal creates, poetry does its dance as a humorous intelligence. Caution: Breuer dances with two left feet.

Breuer's fables are poems for pleasure; entertaining, intelligent, sensual, they are the work of a master ironist. Not to mention a closet esoteric-type who delights in pedagogical humor. In passage after passage of virtuosic uses of metaphor and metonymy, rhetorical devices, macaronic verse, neologisms, sound rhythms, and free associations on verbal and visual ideas, Breuer creates quite dazzling poetry. The animations develop a metalanguage that seems to make itself up as it goes along, surprisingly rich in its imaginative devices and lack of regularity. It is writing about writing. Breuer especially loves language in the context of the speech act. No wonder the animals are all compulsive talkers, forever going on about themselves. By telling their stories, they situate themselves in the world.—"I speak therefore I am." The trilogy is really based on the art of storytelling, a vanishing form in the technological age which, as Walter Benjamin lamented, has substituted mere information-giving for "the ability to exchange experiences." (With what foresight Benjamin prophesied the information-giving nature of contemporary art.)

Breuer's intention is precisely that—to offer experience in the subtle form of corrective comedy. It is not surprising then that his work takes the form of the aphorism so often; the aphoristic style lends itself to offering advice, relating a moral, or commenting satirically with the intent to inform. Breuer's pithy remarks on the state of human affairs are all the more comical coming from the mouths of animals who appear hopelessly and helplessly human in their predicaments. (Like Kafka's mouse Josephine fussing about the relationship of her art to her audience.)

And what wonderfully intelligent creatures these animals are, with their liberated word play, delight in crisscrossing verbal and visual puns, and witty circumlocution. The puns, especially, emphasize the circularity of speech, the result being that ideas and images can be extended virtually infinitely, the verbal interacting with the visual not only in pure madcap fun, but often in highly sophisticated associations. Robert Pincus-Witten identifies a California sensibility in the proclivity toward punning, a fact which is not far-fetched when one considers that Breuer grew up in California and keeps in touch with the West Coast Californians and their playful attitude toward art and artifacts. The pun is the most dominant rhetorical device in the animations.

From a dramatic point of view the most distinctive aspect of the animations is the complete lack of dialogue. Even though other figures may appear (*B.Beaver*, *Shaggy Dog*) or be referred to (*Red Horse*) in the plays, neither discourse nor conflict between characters is dramatized at any time in performance; that is to say, performers do not relate to each other in performance. Think for a moment about the implications of a drama that doesn't dramatize anything: it means that the dramatization of a conflict on stage, the conventional (and even unconventional) definition of drama is completely undermined. My own feeling is that the continued emphasis on the life of the spirit (the holistic approach to life, the integrated personality) and the turning away from rationalist thought may lead us in time—though not the foreseeable future—to a drama which is not based on conflict. Breuer's animations are the touch of a suggestion of this direction.

Breuer's radical conception of dramaturgy disregards the conventional uses of plot, dialogue, setting, time, and character in favor of an open-ended form that has the shape of the prose poem. The idea of passages in a life is substituted for plot, in place of dialogue he puts the monologue, instead of setting he develops the notion of personal space, memory takes over for dramatic time and, as I have already pointed out, the chorus takes the place of the individual character.

Breuer's use of chorus is not thematic or information-giving, as is usually the case, but works as the structural backbone of the animation, reflecting his conception of character in the drama: polyphonic voices substitute for the individual voice. Through the device of the chorus the narration evolves from several perspectives in the metonymic functioning of the actors; the notion of gender doesn't exist, nor does any separation between the past and the present. And, as in Oriental theatre, the voice is separated from the character. The actors as it were take turns enacting events from the animal's life rather than imitating them. Interestingly, Peter Handke's *Sprechstücke* also feature choruses ("speakers") instead of individuated characters, a musical approach to text, literary ready-mades, and lack of dialogue. But the important difference between Breuer and Handke is that the latter creates works which have no visual orientation, while Breuer is interested in motivational action (the emotive gesture) in highly imagistic settings. Notwithstanding, Breuer and Handke share the distinction of having created a few of the most provocative texts for the stage in the last decade.

Yet, the animations are as free-flowing and personal as the *Sprechstücke* are schematic and objective. The poetic monologues that comprise the animations lend themselves to expressivity because they are temporarily unrestricted. The monologue seems to work for Breuer as the natural organizer of his lyrical outpourings. From the perspective of autobiography, the monologues function as mediators of the unconscious. If as Jacques Lacan observes, "the unconscious is the discourse of the Other," then it is the place where Breuer talks to himself.

Though the monologue is the unifying structure of the plays, Breuer relates his fables in a variety of ways. His is not story theatre, however, which is illustrative, but epic theatre, a dialectical one. Extending Bertolt Brecht's ideas about epic acting, the chorus, the autonomy of each theatrical element, and the narrative aspect of the performing space itself, Breuer tells his stories not only literally but musically, filmically, electronically, sculpturally, spatially, diagrammatically, kinetically, photographically, chromatically (not always in the same animation, of course)—all of them functioning as different and autonomous kinds of "writing" in the grammar of the event. Breuer refers to his technique as "tracking": it simply means the laying down of parallel lines of narration. In this way, the background and all elements of staging comment on what the performers, who theatricalize states of being, say and do. In Breuer's narrative strategy all space is semantic; everything in it emphasizes its conception as "writing."

These approaches to narrative link Breuer no doubt with Brechtian aesthetics, but there are other theatrical parallels as well. Perhaps the most obvious influence is Samuel Beckett (by way of James Joyce) whose use of narrative and the monologue, and treatment of consciousness, is unmistakably a presence in the animations. (Breuer's understanding of Beckett is fiercely evident in his brilliant stagings of *Play*, *Come and Go*, and *The Lost Ones*.) One can also see affinities with the work of Gertrude Stein, particularly her emphasis on consciousness and the continuous present, the lack of dialogue, stage directions and individualized characters in her plays, and the announcement of sections of a play within the play itself. This aphorism of Stein's seems profoundly descriptive of the formal arrangement of Breuer's plays on the page: "A sentence is not emotional, a paragraph is."

In a more contemporary American context, Breuer aligns himself with the poets' theatre of Frank O'Hara and Kenneth Koch in their integration of art theories in drama, and the mixing of popular and classical literary forms; theirs, however, is a much more literary approach to theatre than Breuer's. Closer to Breuer's own manipulation of language is that of Sam Shepard; both writers love to play with the "attitude" in various styles of American vernacular speech. Coincidentally, the two (characteristically "California" artists) reflect the liberated poetic style of the Beats, their romanticism and their interest in musicalizing literary texts.

These theatrical and dramatic lines, and modern literary tradition appear side by side with the strong currents from the art world which inform the animations. From *Red Horse* to *B.Beaver* to *Shaggy Dog* one can trace, respectively, a movement from minimalism to process art to super-realism in the execution of the texts. They also connect with the emotional attitude of abstract expressionism (isn't that a style that makes emotion "formal"?), pop art, and the more recent story art (John Baldessari, Bill Beckley, William Wegman), and to a greater extent, the punning and ready-made concepts that descend from Marcel Duchamp, and which are refashioned in the more contemporaneous art of Robert Rauschenberg, Jasper Johns, and Bruce Nauman. Finally, and not the least important, as a sophisticated conceptual theatre Mabou Mines has a long history of collaborating with artists on their productions (Tina Girouard, Jene Highstein, Gordon Matta-Clark); no other theatre group in America can make this claim. (An odd contradiction in Mabou Mines' position vis-à-vis the art world is the fact that while the group is so art-oriented, art world people haven't given them full recognition because they tend to dislike the attempt to use trained performers, preferring instead the untrained.)

What is remarkable about the creation of the animations is their ability to accommodate the most contemporary styles of art with theatrical history and literary tradition, in a form derived from the cartoon! Breuer is among the very few gifted playwriting talents in the post-absurdist theatre. That is quite startling when one considers that he is generally thought of as a director rather than as a playwright, nor are the animations seriously talked about as plays—by the press or the public.

Lee Breuer devised an original concept for the typographical layout of each animation that would express its individuality as a text while at the same time suggesting how it looked in performance. One of the pleasures in reading the animations is following the typographical uniqueness of each play, seeing how each play "thinks."

The dynamism of the texts is captured in capitalization, bold-face type, and the design of certain words or phrases to suggest moods, attitudes, and thematic or structural significance, such as the stutter letters in B.Beaver and Shaggy Dog's "chapter" headings. Overall there is a high iconic quality which reinforces the texts' appearance as poetry, and Breuer's position as an imaginative writer whose writing has a life of its own on the page. It is the kind of writing that incorporates its own written signs as an idiosyncratic grammar.

The intrusion of the photographs from the performance as "inter-texts" makes reading the animations more than a literary experience; one can read the rhetoric of the images, too. Together, then, the text and image interact in a sophisticated performance of their own—the text is theatricalized—relating not on a simple analogical basis but each supplying information the other cannot. Those free spaces which appear where there are no photographs allow the reader time to dream as it were, just as the filled-in (photographic) spaces which "quote" scenes from the performance, allow time to think beyond or along with the image. The "meaning" rests between the text and the image. This gives the reader a creative role in the "making" of the animations, since he must situate himself somewhere between the text and the performance to make the provocative transference between the literal and the metaphorical. The emphasis then shifts from the text to the reader.

Alternating the vertical and horizontal placement of text and photograph creates a challenging dialectic, and transvalues the notion of caption as well. These texts, based on the comic which has been traditionally considered a "low" art form, give the comic book literary respectability, but more to the point, they extend its formal and narrative possibilities while retaining its essential visual idea.

The first play of the trilogy, The Red Horse Animation, is a romance which offers an outline of a narrative, not a complete story, in a tripartite structure: outline, lifeline, storyline. The different lines are not exactly structurally harmonic, but three related approaches to the play. The outline, however, remains the structural basis of Red Horse, and the lifeline and storyline merge after its prologue.

The story purposely fragments the sense of time beginning as the play itself acknowledges, somewhere in the middle. As a narrative mode which derives its aesthetic from the comic book, it clearly tries to "frame" (to arrest) certain moments in the horse's life, without constructing a chronological order. The first third of the play is a taped prologue which suggests the words of a narrator talking out loud as if in a daydream, but when the actors enter the performing space at its conclusion, they take over as both the metaphoric and anthropomorphic image of a horse. They perform the piece for the most part lying down on the performing space which, in painting terms, refers to a canvas, and to extend the allusion further, aligns itself with the abstract expressionist technique of emotionalizing space—the process I referred to earlier as Breuer's formalization of his own emotions.

When the actors take over after the "voice" grows silent, they evolve a choral narrative, each one speaking for the horse. This choral structure reflects the division into three parts of what is really the interior monologue of the only "character" in *Red Horse*, the most isolated, inner-directed world—and the most Beckettian in its intense study of consciousness—depicted in the animations. The play follows the logic of the dream world where the narrator and his idea of a horse become a unified being expressing real emotions. When this happens the outline begins to animate itself.

ROMAN NUMERAL TWO . IN WHICH I THINK I SEE MY SHAPE . This desire to know the landscape of his body—in the sense of both physical and mental terrain—is the compulsive drive of the horse in this journey play of sorts. The narration of the play is linked to the recognition of form so much so that it is spatially organized, developing in its movement a definable geometry of emotion. Form, shape, circle, line: these are the repeated terms of the horse's attempt to trace himself in space. (Coincidentally, these forms reflect the iconic vocabulary of minimalism which has strongly influenced this work in its technical approach.) In the emotional world of *Red Horse* space functions in the form of codes for actual states of being. A circle, therefore, isn't simply a roundness but has to do with circularity in the ontological sense.

When the narrator in the prologue talks about diagramming an outline in blue pencil he draws a knot; with a red pencil he draws a line between some numbers and the shape of a horse appears. Reflecting on his spirit he sees a map, he starts "mapping" consciousness. Now the significance of the play's spatial organization becomes clearer. Travel and distance function not only as literal ideas, but as symbolic and psychological codes, too. (Travel as journey to "inner space" and in the sense of covering "aesthetic" distance.) When the horse begins to construct a history of himself, he evolves a topography of the spirit.

In an autobiographical context, the obsession with form suggests that the narrator is struggling to discover his identity and style as an artist. I'M CHANGING . WHAT AM I . The theme is intricately woven, on the one hand, with the metaphor of freedom and adventure the horse represents and, on the other, with the horse's domestication. These conflicting feelings are purposefully con-fused in parts of the story but coalesce in a dream sequence which features a scene between father and son. The idea of *Red Horse* is that it is about fragmen-tation and contradictory feelings even as it evolves, if only temporarily, as a romance.

The story seems to me full of indecision, ambiguity, doubt, reversing of posi-tions and the sense of impermanence; so much of the intensity of its "present-ness" has to do with its singular focus of an artist, somewhat anguished, trying to find himself yet still having a sense of humor about it (if only as a defensive measure). *Red Horse* does not develop a singular dramatic line (it has three) but offers a variety of narrative approaches in addition to the spatial narration. The story is also told filmically, diagrammatically, musically, metaphorically, chromatically. These different narrative modes do not always synthesize but work in counterpoint as do the play's themes and images, in a deliberate discontinuity of codes.

DO I OWE A DEBT TO THE CINEMA? the horse asks (Capital Letter A), wondering about what may have influenced him; at the same time *Red Horse* itself "thinks" filmically. ELEVEN . SEVEN . GENGHIS KHAN IN-STITUTES THE CRAFT OF DELIVERY . BY HORSE . CUT . PAN OF THE GOBI DESERT . CUT . The "film" depicts the romance of a Mongolian steed, simultaneously uniting the narrator's romantic childhood memory of a film shown in grade school and his subconscious adult feelings about losing his freedom (being domesticated). The horse image has both positive and negative denotations which carry conflicting iconic and symbolic messages.

The horse undergoes a further symbolic transformation in the section which appears as the exposition of a conflict between father and son. One of the more lyrical passages of *Red Horse*, this section finds the horse looking at his reflec-tion in a stream—a pun on the "stream of consciousness"—and remembering his father, Daily Bread, in a dream that flashes by like a movie in his head. One of the reasons why Breuer's autobiographical writings don't remain at the solip-sistic level—this scene especially demonstrates why—is his ability to objectify himself: the horse looks at himself in the stream and a third self looks at the horse looking at the reflection. At the core of the dream, and here the horse ex-periences an epiphany, is the horse's disapproval of his father's obsession with work and making money; the rejection of a bourgeois life style (his father's "domestication") in favor of the bohemian insecurity of an artistic one (his own). If Daily Bread was into "bread" (money) and "circles" (treadmill of suc-cess), his son is into "lines." But in which direction do they point? In the pastoral setting of *Red Horse* (*B.Beaver* and *Shaggy Dog* are urban pieces) the scene is almost elegiac.

If the romance is the traditional form for the wish-fulfillment dream, Breuer subverts the logic of its conventions so that it works in opposition to the out-come of the play. The horse never finds a form he can hold onto but wanders frustrated, goes back to the beginning of the story, and finally loses his sense of self. DON'T KNOW WHAT TO CALL ROMAN NUMERAL SIX . At the end of the story the horse can no longer keep himself together and his image begins to fall apart into space. The narrator's dream is over, and the grim realities of self-doubt come crashing through the frame. *The Red Horse Animation* is Breuer's most poetic, subdued, and reflective work.

In his second animation Breuer introduces B.Beaver, a Job-like figure struggling to build a dam which will secure his house and family. He HAS LOST THE ART OF DAMNATION AT A CRUCIAL TIME B.Beaver tells, in his six-chapter story which moves from the statement of his problem to its resolution. While *Red Horse* exists wholly in the mind of the horse, *B.Beaver* recounts the past; and, unlike the brooding horse, the beaver is a compulsive, stuttering cartoon, the most comical of Breuer's creations.

The story is divided into "text" and "takes." The text is the actual narrative by B.Beaver who acts as a chorus leader while the others he refers to (the brood and the missus) function as a chorus; but whether they are the beaver's mental projections or real family members is not clarified in the text—the beaver is telling his own story. The chorus amplifies aural and visual images of the text with the takes serving as Breuer-as-writer's self-conscious comments on it. The text relates to the past, the takes to the present. The "I" of the story is seen from the perspective of "he" in the takes.

These takes are introduced into the story as literary allusion (B.Beaver is aligned with another comic TURD in dramatic history—Ubu Roi), pop allusion (to the animated cartoon voice of M. MAGOO), free association (on LATIN as related to language and a Puerto Rican social club), cartoon and visual cues (THE DAM COLLAPSES . CURTAINS FLAIL . YIKES . EXPLODES ACROSS THE FRAME .); the text serves to detail character and interpret mood and attitude, too (the last take goofs on the clichés of a sentimental soundtrack).

This emphasis on process has greater significance in the thematic organization of the play itself; in fact, it is its subject. *B.Beaver* is a story about not being able to write, or, being afraid to let writing happen. It is a metaphoric explication on the theme of "writer's block," cleverly disguised in a hilarious story whose lovable hero is a beaver trying to construct a dam (a defense mechanism) so he and his family won't wash away when the snow melts in the spring. (Perhaps I understood this on a purely subconscious level since I was going through the same thing at the time I was beginning to work on this Introduction.) B.Beaver stutters for a very good reason—he can't get the words out. Stuttering is emblematic of his creative problems. In the punning universe that defines *B.Beaver*, you're "damned" if you do, "dammed" if you don't.

The beaver creates all sorts of distractions to deny his creative urge. He gets sidetracked on pedagogical thoughts about geological formations, writes a postcard with a request for "how to" books on building dams; floating downstream he daydreams happy thoughts of escape, twirling his tail around a tree branch he hangs upside down contemplating his dilemma. In one of his fantasies he finds a waterlogged craft and pretends he is captain of a ship, mixing nautical and boxing language for a pun on the idea of creativity. B.Beaver has his serious moments, too; swimming past some workers along the brook bank, he observes: LOOK AT THEM . . . EAT . CRAP . SCREW . CROAK . He refuses "death on the installment plan."

The observation has more than pictorial ramifications because it expands upon the important section from *Red Horse* which explores the philosophical differences of father and son. Here again in the second part of the trilogy the opposition to the banality of the workaday world surfaces. It seems to me that the narrator hasn't resolved the conflict between wanting security for his family, but not wanting to trade the insecurity of the artist's life for a dreary bourgeois life-style. Though family-centered plays have traditionally dominated American drama, this has not been the case in experimental theatre. An exception to this generalization is the animations which feature as an important theme the acceptance of parental responsibility: central to the trilogy is the conflict between a writer wanting to feel free to follow his creative impulses while at the same time wanting to fulfill his responsibilities as a father. As subject matter in an avant-garde context this is pretty rare. (On the other hand, that Breuer is one of the few people in the avant-garde theatre who has a family easily accounts for his concerns.) Not surprisingly, two of the animals he chooses to tell his stories are "domesticated" (horse and dog), the third is involved in defending his home (beaver).

If on the metaphorical level *B.Beaver* acts as a fable about the artist, on the mythical level it demolishes myths about the male "animal" in society. The beaver is continually constructing defenses, and experiencing anxiety and fear about his impulses. He is hiding behind the dam and the desire to keep his family together, afraid of his own creative responses to the world around him. Breuer distorts the portrait of the artist as a confident young man conquering new creative territory for himself.

The story of the uptight beaver is told in a variety of ways that mix Latin, naval language, and clichés with the argot of sports, science, meteorology, algebra, and biology. The different kinds of speech express the frequent transformations in states of mind experienced by the beaver. The imagery, too, reinforces the play's psychological themes.

The most obvious symbol is the dam which, stationary, holds back the creative flow and, washed away, lets creativity come gushing forth. There are other images more tied to nature which, in the deeper structure of the story, become a metaphor for artistic struggle as one of survival against the elements (the beaver hunts salmon instead of the white whale, though). The snow, this massive pure blankness, is a "block" which when thawed will let the creative juices flow, while water itself is the temporary setting for the beaver's floating dreams. In the scheme of things is it any wonder that after the winter and with the coming of spring, the beaver makes his breakthrough? Breuer's use of symbols rests fairly traditionally in his radically-conceived play.

One of the joys of Breuer's writing is its sensual quality. *Shaggy Dog* is the animation about sexual attitudes, but *B.Beaver* has its own special erotics. When the beaver is finally on the verge of accepting his creative impulses he grows excited sexually and has an erection: he prepares "to come" into his own as an artist. In this way writing is associated with orgasm on the physiological level, and with the building of a structure, on the physical. (Regarding this last point, the notion of creating art as making a work—physical labor—is very much in the vocabulary of contemporary artists in all fields, as if they feel the need, as Americans in a country which values manual labor and devalues artistic labor, to justify their activities as work.)

In *The B.Beaver Animation* Breuer has created a very sophisticated cartoon about being a writer: a genuinely funny, self-effacing work that proves how unpretentious an artist Breuer is. The sort who would stub his toe on a statue of the muse. Breuer's witty union of sexual and intellectual humor in exaggerated settings construed to emphasize human foibles make him the Groucho Marx of the American avant-garde.

Breuer's gifts as an imaginative writer create a striking presence in *The Shaggy Dog Animation*. Now, in this animation, five times longer than any other, he creates the space for his soul to sing. The voice belongs to a dog called Rose, and sing she does—a torch song about her man that got away. The story of a filmmaker/dog Rose, *Shaggy Dog* is a bittersweet soap opera with a cast of characters who include, besides Rose and another dog Broadway, a rabbit, Bunny, and two humans, John and Leslie, all of whom appear in a series of adventures that unravel in California, Las Vegas, and New York. It is a love story that makes fun of love, mocking its illusions, pain, sentimentality and foolishness, while acknowledging its supreme ecstasy. Sounds like the definition of "puppy love."

Shaggy Dog is all reflecting surfaces, electronic perfection, artificial emotion: romance as fabricated in movies and sung about in popular songs. To get at the craziness of his subject Breuer musicalizes the text in performance, using different kinds of musical styles for the "attitude" they embody, so that *Shaggy Dog* becomes at times talking rock, with all sound filtered through the sophisticated stereophonic equipment that manipulates the voices of nine performers who speak for Rose in solo, trio, and choral form. I don't wish to deal with performance per se—that's not my focus here—but it is necessary to know the basic set-up of the play to understand Breuer's canny remark to an interviewer: "You can't say 'I love you' anymore without an echo chamber . . . [it] has captured the myth of the expression more clearly than the human voice." Music so dominates contemporary notions of romance that people identify experience with the musical theme it suggests to them. Rose tells John in her special idiolect: HOW LONG . HAD I LONGED . TO SING THE SONG . THAT PLUGGED YOUR PRONG . INTO MY SOCKET . AND THERE IT WAS . SWEETS . KINKY REGGAE .

Shaggy Dog is the perfect piece for the disco age. Slick, controlled, stylish, and synthetic. It has to do with performance: in the sense of the performing self, and in relation to definitions of metatheatre. In the world Breuer creates characters act out ideal romantic images of themselves in a glossy setting, decorated with the gadgetry of a technological society. Never mind a Saturday night fever, Rose is in heat.

The play's slickness characterizes avant-garde theatre now, as opposed to ten years ago when technology wasn't so prominent in it, and the more advanced theatre had a homemade, "poor" quality. *Shaggy Dog* is "rich" in more ways than one: it represents more sophisticated theatrical conceptualization as well as more money available for experimentation. The movement from *Red Horse* (minimalism) to *Shaggy Dog* (post-minimalism) has been to progressively more color and technological equipment. In *Shaggy Dog* style is subject.

A "Love Story" for the avant-garde, *Shaggy Dog* is based entirely on the clichés of romance as it is depicted in popular mythology, and propagated by the mass media. When Rose and John make love on a California beach A WAKI LUA LANI KALOA KALUA MOON surfs over them; John (a filmmaker himself) creates cinematic illusions of his affairs with Leslie (I REMEMBER ONCE PROJECTING A PLACE IN THE SUN ONTO LESLIE). Not only are there puns on and allusions to songs and film (these are used throughout the production), but to television (Kojak is on Rose's "telly") and to consumer products (A HOBART 700 SPEED QUEEN DISHWASHER sits in her kitchen). It's the innocence of pop art updated in the detached cool of super-realism: a "California" (in sensibility and in place) love story according to pop culture.

Shaggy Dog takes the form of an extended "Dear John" letter from the narrator Rose (a puppet as well as a dog) to John (her owner) in which she reflects on their relationship which ended three years ago (twenty one in the dog's cycle). It works itself out in a binary structure of "sound track" in which the actual narrative unfolds (the subjective line) and "image track" in which the text comments on itself (the objective line), the two tracks together evolving as a fugue.

The story itself is basically very simple though it takes an incredibly circumlocuitous path to its unraveling—it is a shaggy dog story: prologue (a kind of radio play which takes place before the image track appears in the text); Part I in which Rose recalls the high points of her love affair; Part II in which John and Rose break up; Part III, three years after the affair. The animation follows virtually a classical narrative line: a heroine comes to know the truth about herself by going through a series of meaningful experiences. Of course, these experiences are not dramatized, only recalled by Rose.

In essence, Rose moves from feeling I WAS THE DIMENSION OF THE SHADOWY SPACE FROM ONE SHOE TO ANOTHER (her first meeting with John) to MY LIFE HAS CHANGED . IT'S TAKEN A TRULY IN-WARD TURN . MY FEELINGS HAVE BECOME THE FACTS . . . AND OUTSIDE I FELT SO PROFOUND I CONTROLLED THE WEATHER (Rose has an epiphany in the snow) to GOODBYE . DEAR . I SAID . AND SANK INTO THE NIGHT LIKE A PIECE OF BACON IN THE BOWL OF SPLIT PEA SOUP (the corny simile wonderfully props up Rose's cool resolve to go her own way). By the last few pages of the play Rose has become fully militant, quoting Lautréamont's *Maldoror* in a passage about dogs who break their chains and run madly through the countryside, unable to control their new-found freedom. *Shaggy Dog* traces the movement of the soul toward liberation; in Rose's case, the development of a feminist consciousness.

A work I don't think would have been possible without the influence of the women's movement, *Shaggy Dog* is a mature feminist statement of remarkable metaphoric and philosophic richness. It demonstrates the awakening of consciousness in a series of ironic events that are both humorous and profoundly moving and, even more significant, it reflects a movement away from the more self-absorbed earlier animations to a much broader social context.

Yet, there is much more to *Shaggy Dog* than the contemporaneity of its feminism. As an artist Rose acts as a metaphor for Breuer's own feelings about being an artist. But she is also a puppet, physically manipulated in performance by performers (male and female) who are in turn manipulated by a sound system, a concrete allusion to her emotional manipulation by John (the image track studies the problem as it relates to the MECHANISM OF ATTACH-MENT). As an abstract idea the puppet refers to the aesthetics of Bunraku which is an art based on the idea of storytelling through music, and further-more, a theatrical mode which separates the narration into three separate "tracks" as it were: singer, puppet, manipulators.

And just as Rrose (a Rose is a Rose is a Rose) Selavy represents Duchamp's feminine nature (even as a name "Rose" has mythological status), so she is emblematic of the narrator's view as expressed in the clichés of an oppressed minority, a view encompassing both androgyny and metamorphosis. This very special Rose is a dog owned by a master—the metaphor for the narrator's perception of the artist enslaved (owned by) the art world. Metaphor is clearly the organizing principle of the animations, more complexly in *Shaggy Dog* than the others, because here metaphors are doubled in Rose's status as both dog and artist.

The real coup of *Shaggy Dog* is that Rose is so believable as a human being and artist, in a narrative that offers the multiple perspectives of the "I" who tells the story and the "they" who comment on it without involving them as writers. The irony of the image track keeps the reader from falling into the sentimentality that the story is constantly bouncing off of in the sound track. To make matters more complicated in this already beautifully complicated story, there is also a film metaphor to suggest that *Shaggy Dog* is a movie that John and Rose are separately evolving in their heads. John (a shooter) and Rose (a cutter) get confused as to who's in whose scenario. Early on in the story Rose comments: ME AND MY MOVIE . WE WENT INTO PRODUCTION . ALL MY LINES CAME TRUE . It came together for Rose and John in Venice. With Leslie off making a commercial, they wander off to the beach, make love and dream in a scene which depicts the most total convergence of animal and human species in the animations. Here is a sample of Rose's poetry:

WE'LL PICK UP DISEASES . AND FOAM AT THE MOUTH AND GET THIN AND CIVILIZED LIFE WILL SHUN OUR KIND . THEY'LL CALL OUT THE CATCHERS . BUT WE'LL ESCAPE . PAST SANTA BARBARA . PAST SAN LUIS OBISBO . PAST GOR- DA . SPECIAL PEOPLE WILL AID AND ABET US . ROMANTIC PEOPLE . THEY'LL BLOW KISSES FROM SPORTS CARS AND BECKON US TO THEIR BEACH BLANKETS WHERE THEY'LL TOAST OUR HEALTH IN A TEQUILA SUNRISE RIGHT OUT OF A THERMOS .

This passage includes all of the most characteristic features of the animation in general: clichés of popular romance, parodistic humor and imagery, motifs of Romanticism, California sensibility, poetic language, fantasy.

Alas, back in civilization love starts to fade and Rose and John drift apart. Sick with grief Rose overeats, throws temper tantrums when John is with Leslie, takes a new lover, Bunny—all of the things humans do to compensate for a broken heart. But by the end of Part II Rose no longer needs John and she leaves him on a New York street at 4:00 a.m. while they're out for a walk. Rose is liberated, now it's John's turn to suffer. Breuer creates a tour de force scene in Part III which shows a distraught John, now a "puppet" himself, simultaneously dialing John's Anonymous and a girlfriend:

WHAT CAN I DO . I GO INTO MYSELF . I BECOME SELF IN- VOLVED . I TRY TO BE SELF EFFACING . BUT THAT'S SELF DEFEATING . I INDULGE IN SELF RECRIMINATION . BUT ALL THAT DOES IS MAKE ME MORE SELF CENTERED .

Breuer is relentless in this satirical "closeup" of John which makes fun of current self-help jargon and reverses the position of the male in the relationship.

Meanwhile, Rose is on the sound track admitting that she misses John: even with age (Rose is now twenty-one years older) one never loses illusions about love. SING ME A CHORUS OF CHERRY PIE ... I TELL YOU THE TRUTH . ONLY SLEEPING DOGS LIE . Rose ends *Shaggy Dog* quoting a song and a cliché—the twin foundations of a love relationship.

Shaggy Dog evolves a style which I think of as "Quotation Art": bolstered by the ironic stance of the artist it is a way of creating art from the clichés and conventions embodied in the intellectual and emotional patterns of a given society. Quotation Art embraces the literary ready-made, a narrative strategy not without its striking examples here and in Europe. Peter Handke's *Sprechstücke* come readily to mind with Robert Wilson's *A Letter for Queen Victoria* which took much of its language, not from officialese, maxims, slogans, and advertisements as Handke did, but from television programming, and Sam Shepard's *Tooth of Crime* whose dialogue is filled with the argot of the rock, sports, crime, and business worlds. In each of these examples artists have taken the vernacular of their society and turned it back on itself—Handke for political purposes; Breuer, Wilson, and Shepard for more mythic strategies. The idea of Quotation Art is that it is an art rooted in signs: it moves all imagery and language in multiple directions, with the signifier continually becoming the signified. *Shaggy Dog* transmits Breuer's ideas about the ways in which the individual is socialized (programmed) by his/her internalization of popular mythology in a series of different codes (aural, symbolic, iconic, musical, linguistic, etc.) by which culture functions as a language.

Claude Lévi-Strauss's definition of the creation of myth from the "remains and debris of events . . . odds and ends . . . fossilized evidence of the history of an individual or a society" is provocative in this context. Mythical thought as "an intellectual form of 'bricolage.' " If anything, Breuer's quotation of certain American mythologies is a recycling of the junk of an advanced technological society to create a form which acts as a critique of that society. *Shaggy Dog* is love among the ruins.

Shaggy Dog works at the level of critique because it satirizes, instead of simply mocking, popular culture, a position which reinforces its moral underpinning. (Conversely, Theatre of the Ridiculous, a style also built on the clichés of popular culture and its entertainments, doesn't work as critique because it always remains at the level of parody; it becomes nostalgic, campy.) Though the piece plays with schlock imagery, Breuer's critical intelligence keeps it from becoming kitsch.

The morality of form I think is clear in the spatial poetics delineated in Rose's living quarters, and which is identified in the image track. For example, the bathroom is identified as the place of pride; the kitchen is the scene of hate; the den is the seat of power. Working with the notion of behavior in a particular space Breuer designates special areas for the "sins" lovers commit. While Rose is making creme puffs (one of Breuer's idiosyncratic puns) in her kitchen, the image track guided by the voices of the speakers is telling her: DON'T LAUGH ROSE . THE WORD IS . HATE . "Interior decoration" is equated with Rose's state of mind. Functioning in this way, the rooms go beyond being environments and move toward the concept of theological space. If *Shaggy Dog* isn't quite a "divine comedy," it is a comedy of manners with a moral persuasion: a parable in the manner of Kafka. Though Breuer probably didn't have topoanalysis (Bachelard's term) in mind, it seems likely his ideas about the behavioral aspects of space were influenced by the artist Gordon Matta-Clark who worked on part of *Shaggy Dog*'s design. In any case, this sensitivity to behavior and space is a concern one can trace in the work of such artists as Vito Acconci, Bruce Nauman, Robert Smithson, and Mel Bochner to name a few, while at the same time being another example of Breuer's familiarity with current art theory.

Rose's own sojourn into the art world—she does it because she has to support her litter (here again the theme of parental responsibility that runs through the animations)—is humorously chronicled in Part I of the play. Now she satirizes art, patrons, critics, and grantsmanship:

I LEARNED TO SHAKE HANDS . PLAY DEAD . AND BEG . TWO WEEKS LATER I PICKED UP A CAPS GRANT .

While these lines follow on the sound track, the image track, which relates to it both contrapuntally and analogically, puns on SEE YOURSELF AS A HEAVYWEIGHT as Muhammed Ali's physical measurements are listed. This is typical of the way the humor of the piece grows out of the eccentric wedding of metaphors in the two tracks. And in this case, the way humor plays with the imagery: THE SCENE OF YOUR BOMBER JACKET DRAPED ON A PRESTO LOG . IN A FIELD OF LEFTOVER RAVIOLI . COURTESY RAUSCHENBERG . Much of the fun of *Shaggy Dog* rests with the reader's capacity to understand its references which they can only do by being part of a certain society or group. The link is anthropological.

Rose soon tires of the "sub rosa" tactics of the art world and decides to leave it; for her, it's an act of liberation. It is no surprise that Rose is the only one of the animals in the animations who has a name; she is the only one with a clear idea of her selfhood. In an autobiographical sense, the animations move from *Red Horse*, which has to do with self-definition, and *B.Beaver*, with the acceptance of creative impulses, to *Shaggy Dog*, which portrays an artist with a clear idea of self and art. In other words, a shift from self criticism to a criticism of the system that represents a ten year development in the consciousness of a writer. *The Shaggy Dog Animation* brings together all the techniques and themes of the trilogy in a work of stunning lyrical beauty and depth of perception whose authenticity of emotion is quite extraordinary.

In the animations Lee Breuer has created a language that only the animations know and whose narrator is known only to them. It is the language of an imagination at once seductive, witty, eccentric, and enormously aware of how writing prompts thinking. The animations reject a bourgeois value system based on the demands of a consumer culture and the dramaturgy it creates to reflect itself. And they reject the notion of a reader consumed by the text in favor of one who can collaborate in its making by allowing another "culture" to grow from it. The result is writing that provides space for the imagination to play in, in the play each reader imagines.

[1979]

Peter Handke's
My Foot My Tutor
Aspects of Modernism

SINCE HIS THEATRICAL DEBUT IN 1966 WITH THE CONTROVER-
sial *Offending the Audience,* Peter Handke has been recognized as a major contemporary writer in the West. His literary roots in drama extend from Horvath
and Brecht to Beckett and Ionesco, and in the novel from Dostoevsky and
Kafka to Beckett and Robbe-Grillet. To date, the thirty-five-year-old Austrian
has published a remarkable number of plays, novels, poems, and essays which
signal him as one of the most important young writers of his generation. While
only a few of Handke's fictional works have appeared in English, the plays of
this former Gerhart Hauptmann Prize for Drama winner (1967-1968), are now
available to the American public, and one volume of his poetry has been
translated. Richard Gilman's recent *The Making of Modern Drama* begins with
Georg Büchner and ends with Peter Handke.

Handke's body of work is chiefly concerned with language and behavior, a
major interest with central European writers. His five *Sprechstücke* (*Offending
the Audience, Self-Accusation, Quodlibet, Prophecy, Calling for Help*), which are
termed "speak-ins" by his translator, Michael Roloff, have as their subject the
acquisition of language and its influence on behavior. These "speak-ins,"
Handke's own dramatic creations, are consciousness-raising pieces which attempt to make the audience aware not only of the theatre experience, but life
experience. As such they are didactic in the broadest sense of the term, though
in no way are they as doctrinaire as Brecht's *Lehrstücke* to which they defer.

Kaspar, perhaps Handke's most praised play, is a major dramatic work of the
contemporary theatre. Drawing on the absurdist influences of Beckett and
Ionesco it is, nevertheless, Handke's personal critique of society which regulates
reality by means of its language structure. In it Handke attempts to show his

audience the difference between a world shaped by consciousness and one burdened by platitudes.

Any serious playwright writing in the German language is forced necessarily to undergo a comparison between himself and Bertolt Brecht, if not technically, at the very least in terms of engagement. Handke's plays resemble Brecht's dramaturgically in their "estrangement" of the audience, their use of a nonliterary language, popular forms of entertainment, and social gestus. Significantly, however, the dramaturgy of Handke and Brecht is comparable more in its means than its ends.

Handke has consistently refused to use the drama for his own political statements, or to demonstrate solutions to political problems. Thus, his sense of engagement is contrary to that of Brecht and Brecht's successor, Peter Weiss. Handke is interested only in offering to an audience a new consciousness of reality—as it is, not as it should be. In an essay entitled "Brecht, Play, Theatre, Agitation" the young playwright has written:

> The theatre as a social institution seems to me useless as a way of changing social institutions. The theatre formalizes every moment, every insignificant detail, every word, every silence; it is no good at all when it comes to suggesting solutions.

According to Handke, committed theatre is not possible in the theatre. It exists elsewhere—in the street, in the university.

Handke, who is an avowed Marxist, has been repeatedly accused of "formalism," "apoliticism," and "bourgeois false consciousness" by leftist audiences and critics. When his play without words, My Foot My Tutor, was first performed in Germany in 1969, it was criticized as an example of "blind literature" by audiences who missed its subtle variations on the theme of domination and submission.

The play has more to do with what Handke refers to as "pre-political sensations"—those feelings which eventually lead to political acts. My Foot My Tutor is concerned with behavior and attitude; it focuses on surface realities and the ordinary poses of the indivudual.

In My Foot My Tutor surfaces and appearances are of utmost importance. Handke's theatrical exploration of non-linguistic modes of communication and presentation provides a sensory experience rarely accessible in today's theatre. That the theatrical text of this play is semiotic rather than verbal, compels one to concentrate on movements, sounds, and gestures. My Foot My Tutor, like all modernist works, demands of its audiences an alternative, radical way of approaching the theatre event.

My Foot My Tutor is a highly stylized silence play (or, play without words) comprised of ten scenes which are variations on a central theme: power. The play has a dramatic antecedent in Beckett's one character tragicomedy, Act

Without Words, but it is more radical in that it features two characters. In a series of mutation scenes which occur in a farm setting Handke articulates by means of movement and sound the relationship between two men, the Ward and the Warden, in which the Warden is the dominant figure. The multiple choices of meaning—political, social, aesthetic—subtly exposed in the play are varied and variable; it is an exercise in metaphors.

Handke's wordless, plotless play which articulates every action in great detail, exists in the realm of pure naturalism, inviting the audience to investigate with great awareness all of its non-semantic elements: movement, sound, music and light. However, for the fullest understanding of the play's technical and textural richness, a careful reading of the script is necessary.

This is a paradoxical point because the very theatricality of the piece rests in its playable qualities. Still, the text is capable of providing an intellectual stimulation that would be difficult, if not impossible, to duplicate on stage.

My Foot My Tutor illustrates Handke's fascination with the act of creation. That the playwright's enthusiasm has sired a kind of literary authoritarianism is evident in his anticipation, and at times coercion, of the reader's "justifiable" reaction. The text at one point reads, "Can one gather from the manner in which the Ward consumes the apple that he enjoys dependent status?" "Actually not" is the textual reply. This is Handke's interpretation of the action, i.e., the proper interpretation.

The text specifies directions for the presentation of the play and directives to the audience/reader concerning the most comprehensible approach to it. Like Handke's earlier "speak-in," *Offending the Audience*, it is written virtually as a dialogue with the audience. In the American theatre, only the experimentalist Richard Foreman (Ontological-Hysteric Theater) is as consciously concerned with his audience. Like Handke's speak-ins, his plays are confrontations with the audience in which the dialectic is played out, not on the stage, but in the relationship between stage and audience. His productions include taped directives and voice-overs which skillfully manipulate audience response and suggest ways to observe events on stage. In this respect, they might be considered "teach-ins."

Early on in *My Foot My Tutor* Handke establishes an observing technique by which one learns to be responsive to the play's non-verbal elements. This fundamentally cinematic technique compels the viewer to deflect his eyes from the gravitational center of the action and to focus instead on other events and objects in the same scene. "If we first paid too much attention to the figure, we now have sufficient time to inspect the other objects and areas," Handke notes in the text, in an attempt to stimulate sensory perception.

In the expository first scene of the play, Handke introduces many of the techniques used in subsequent scenes. He indicates, meticulously and nondescriptively, the objects and events on stage ("The person wears no covering on his head"; "We see that he is wearing hobnail boots"). He acknowledges the illusion of theatre ("We see that the Ward is leaning with his back against the backdrop representing the house wall"). The Wittgensteinian tenor of the line, "The cat represents what it does," alerts an audience to the realization that objects are to be determined by their function on stage. In other words, objects on stage do not necessarily function as they do in reality.

Handke also calls attention to the producedness of the play (his *Offending the Audience* is entirely about the theatre and the theatre-goer) by referring intermittently to the props on the stage, to the introduction or withdrawal of light or music in a scene. Also, the two actors in the play wear masks which "estrange" them from the audience, and objectify the theatrical experience for the spectator.

All of Handke's work for the theatre is concerned with language and behavior. His "speak-in," *Self-Accusation*, shows the socialization of an individual through his acquisition of language. A later play, *Kaspar*, in which the hero is mentally destroyed by his knowledge of language, carries the notion of language as an instrument of communication to its absurdist conclusions. Like Ionesco, Handke believes that language is incapable of functioning as an absolute mode of communication.

In *My Foot My Tutor* Handke disregards language as a prerequisite system of meaning by eliminating words altogether in favor of a semiotic text. In the nonverbal world of sound, gesture, and movement are to be found the suggestions for meaning in the play, and the variations of the play's themes. The play is, in effect, a series of tropisms.

Handke substitutes physicalization for language, in the process muting the normal boundary between word and gesture. The crunch of an apple; the grating of a chair pushed away from a table; the rip of a piece of paper; footsteps growing progressively louder—these sounds have a subtlety all their own, and evoke, at times, a Pinteresque mood, or the mood of a detective film. The scratching of an arm, the lift of a foot, a squat, a kick—these are actions capable of furnishing the audience with an aural-visual, and kinesthetic, experience. The absence of words frees one to observe, to be affected by, the non-verbal aspects of *My Foot My Tutor* which is as much an evocation of an environment as a play.

My Foot My Tutor examines the banality of ordinary actions, just as the *Sprechstücke* concern themselves with the platitudes of speech. The minimalist technique employed by Handke exposes both man and object as subjects for observation, as though theatre were a laboratory. Man becomes a specimen under a microscope, to be focused in close-up, medium shot, long shot. Handke's language is sparse and unequivocal, without stylistic flourishes, unemotive. There is only what is; nothing more, nothing less. To quote Heidegger: "The human condition is to be there."

My Foot My Tutor is Handke's most eclectic work for the theatre, borrowing heavily from artistic and scientific developments. The play reflects the technical innovations of progressive music, film, art, and the novel while also revealing a scientific orientation.

The concept of subtraction is a dominant feature of the play. Continuing in the direction of many artistic modernists, Handke has "subtracted" himself from his work, and become an objective reporter of events instead. As avant-garde composers rebelled against the tyranny of the music score, Handke (for the production of the play) has rebelled against the tyranny of the dramatic text. Hence, the subtraction of dialogue.

Psychological reference to the Ward and Warden is also lacking in the play. The impersonality of the characters makes it impossible to define them in psychological-historical terms. The characters inhabit a world of the continuous present; they have no past. The play manifests movement minus time, sound minus language, character minus personality. The barren landscape of the play emphasizes the void that defines the lives of the two men, alone in a farmhouse away from civilization.

Handke's method of constructing the scenario for the production approximates cinematic technique. His approach is that of a film director who is setting up a "shot." One may think of the entire play as a series of "shots" or stills ("A new scene now begins in the dark, we can hear it"). In the style of film-makers who often refer to other films in their own (Godard, for example), Handke explains the action of a scene. His use of Country Joe McDonald's instrumental piece, "Colors for Susan," provides a mysterious, ponderous effect not unlike that produced by the intermittent striking of baroque chords on an organ in Alain Resnais's film, *Last Year at Marienbad*. The expressive quality of the music suggests a change of events and a change of mood while also strengthening Handke's pronounced ties to the rock movement (his "rules for the actors" which precedes *Offending the Audience* orders the performers to listen to certain Beatles and Rolling Stones songs).

Handke makes it understood that one should think of his text in cinematic terms. A line in the text reads:

> During the period without movement we just listen to the music. Now the music becomes nearly inaudible just as the main theme may disappear almost entirely during sections of a film.

In *The Ride Across Lake Constance* Handke goes farther in his exploration of cinematic expression and objects in the space-time continuum. The characters in this play are given the names of actual German actors and actresses (Emil Jannings, Elizabeth Bergner, and others) which pinpoints the frame of reference. If Handke borrows from the cinema, he also quotes from the contemporary novel. The text of *My Foot My Tutor* is written in the manner of a novel, a continuous body of sentences and paragraphs, narrative in form. It reflects the anguish of Beckettian characters and the minimal technique of both

Beckett and Robbe-Grillet. Influenced by the French new novel and the new cinema of Antonioni, Resnais, Straub, Handke's main occupation in *My Foot My Tutor* is the meticulous narration of surface realities. His novels demonstrate the same techniques, and show the same concerns for the existential realities of his characters.

In addition to cinematic and literary influences, the play has a scientific base, namely in its reliance on probability. But, it is important to note that an audience unfamiliar with Handke's technique or the written text of the play will find it virtually impossible to distinguish between determinability and indeterminability. The problem is the same for avant-garde music when chance compositions are performed. Only those familiar with the music or theory of the composer can understand the role of chance in the music performance.

"Objects either break or they don't"; ". . . the Ward throws a thistle which hits the Warden's chest (or not)"; "The figure on the stage is young—some recognize that this figure probably represents the Ward"—these textual references are the literary counterparts of mathematical theories of probability which are rarely explored in contemporary theatre. The tautological structure of the play—for instance, "see above" is a textual directive, ditto marks appear four times under a line in the text—mirrors the mathematical principle of infinity, and infinite sets of numbers, a concept often examined in modern art, poetry, and music, but not in theatre.

There are other features which reflect the play's focus on time (stasis). The hopelessness of the Ward's situation is exemplified by a scene in which he has a nosebleed (the text reads "Fadeout" then, "end of scene"). "The Warden is sitting there by himself, the Ward doesn't budge from the spot, doesn't budge from the spot. . . . " The frozen picturalization fixes the scenic interpretation: the situation will persist ad infinitum. The Ward is leading a "still life." He is in an advanced state of entropy; his literary counterparts include many of the most famous characters in modern literature, among them those created by Kafka, Sartre, Camus, Beckett. The time metaphor is reinforced in other scenes: the ripping off of the pages of a calendar (the passage of time in cinema is often expressed in this way), the echo of a beet cutting machine, and the fitting Beckettian image at the end of the play—sand slipping through the fingers of the Ward. *My Foot My Tutor* is, in effect, Handke's *Endgame*.

In *My Foot My Tutor* Peter Handke has gone farther than any other contemporary experimental playwright in his exploration of behavior patterns in the interactions of individuals. By stripping away dialogue, he gives us only the image, forcing us to see—to confront—two men enacting a series of metaphors of contemporary reality. It is their silent ritual that "speaks" to us in a language we of the twentieth century can recognize . . . to our misfortune.

[1977]

The Other Lillian Hellman

> It goes without saying that in their
> memoirs people should try to tell
> the truth as they see it or else
> what's the sense? Maybe time blurs
> or changes things for them. But
> you try, anyway.
>
> [*Maybe*]

THAT TENACITY AND SENSE OF STRUGGLE IS WHAT I REMEMBER
most about Lillian Hellman from the months I attended her classes. What she
said about theatre, it never was much anyway, didn't stay with me. But I can
still hear the texture of her gravelly voice when she would speak about a "good
writer," how her *w* came crashing down on the *r* in the splendid rush of feeling
for that luxurious state of being. Frankly, when I thought of writers I love I did
not think of her, the work had fallen into place alongside the other silent *h*'s in
my bookshelves. But coming upon her recent *Maybe*, a book as honest in its
uncertainty as a book can be, made me go back and re-read her plays and
memoirs. Now it became perfectly clear that there were two almost completely
different Lillian Hellmans, though I had already begun to suspect as much. The
plays showed how one turns thought into action, the memoirs the turning
back, after having acted, into thought.

The one most known is the dramatist whose style of realism fell under the influence of Ibsen, the frosty Norwegian presence who died one year after she was
born into an altogether different climate, in all senses of the word. In those

days who else was a self-righteous young woman to learn from? Solid well-made prose, like sturdy cross beams in houses of the period, supported the structures of her staunch monuments to moral authority, their foundations laid by weighty social issues. Characters shaped the circumstances of their lives and when their moral judgment was suspect it reflected in the way events turned out, not well. Nothing ever simply happened to Hellman's characters, they did things to themselves.

In this world of absolutes Truth, Morality and Justice were undebatable, Life and Action had purpose, clear meaning. It was a reconstruction of "reality" that assumed what existed in the world could be mastered if one understood the psychology of motivation, if one had strength of will to defy circumstance, and courage to oppose evil. There was a fixed hierarchy of values in the process of socialization. Yes, Hellman was an Ibsenite, but the other writer in her, flamboyantly opposite, has been steadily exposing the illusions in the structures of experience the master builder in her styled.

Just as Ibsen in his later years let the fourth wall of his settings dissolve in an avalanche of ambiguous imagery, no longer confident in the logic of rationalism, or the world and its ways, the later Hellman, too, and now more generous a writer because of it, marvels at the awesome unpredictability of human affairs, the mysterious bonds of certain relationships, seems even to revel in the quirky turns the mind takes as it mixes up illusion and the real, memory and fact, autobiography and fiction. Since she left the theatre Hellman's writing has developed a sense of play that was never in the plays.

They were the work of someone who had thought once that answers were obvious if one asked the right questions, who searched hard for truth and meaning when often none was to be found. Hellman the playwright believed that if one were a healthy person, morally and socially, he or she was assured of a rightful place in the social order. It was left to the other Hellman to show that no matter what some people did there was no place for them in the world we live in, indeed the idea of a Christian universe was itself a myth. The younger writer understood how the world works, the older one finds it impossible to understand. I suppose when one is young the answers are important, and as one ages it is the question that shapes thought.

Why is it that drama ages in a way no other writing does? Are a crowd of people talking so different from a single voice? Or is it the empty space a play is created to fill that makes us so aware its life is only publicly lived, in measured time, that alludes to its death even as it sits artlessly on pages sadly framing the invisible characters and their expressions, like a proscenium arch opening onto an empty stage set in the middle of a day? How much the human body ages through dramatic ages. Why are the snapping turtles of Hellman's Pleasantville farm, the trees and flowers she planted there, and the chickens she raised, more alive to me than her little foxes, her toys in the attic? Wouldn't you choose Julia instead of Regina if you wanted to know any of her women?

The most social of art forms, openly vulnerable and dependent on the tone of voice and gestures of its day, overly obsessive in its need for representation, wanting totally to create the world on a stage, theatre was finally too elaborately culture-bound an art for the independent Hellman who never really was fulfilled by theatre's demands. Drama alluded to the culture in her, the memoirs remarked on her nature, and together they conspired to show how the relationship beween the public and private worlds of a writer could suggest a new dialogue for the part Hellman plays in her writing. All the finely-crafted deceptions in the way realistic drama thinks about itself are laid bare, mocked even, in the relentless inquiry of her memoir style, her drama's critic.

Dramatic form, so insistent on creating a world out of an idea, trapped Hellman in her own box sets that supposed a natural, even proper, order of things, when all the while she was at home in the unruly world outside that is hopelessly open-ended, incomprehensible, unjust. It was left to her auto-biographical writings, always threatening us with their fictional wiliness, to liberate her from her own good sense, to make her the unfinished woman, the woman who has come undone, exchanged the burden of fact for the pleasure of memory (a very special stage in the mind), righteousness for critical doubt, reality for the real. Where once she tried to uncover truth, she later discovered that there rarely is any, preferring instead the contradictions, this woman whose work encompasses her century's welcome of the new realism, and later its revolt against it. If drama is the prose of her life, the memoir is her poetry. Hellman has moved from tragedy to comedy and let the wonderful light of ambiguity in. But she had to stop writing for actors and become a performer in her own scenarios, then move the dialogue from other characters on a stage, to the different stages of her own life. The best dialogue she ever wrote was not between characters, it was between her divided selves, the characters she was or wanted to be.

The Lillian Hellman who ends one book with however, begins another with maybe, and in the one in between, studies the pentimenti of half-remembered images—what is fact? how does time decorate the mind?—is a writer at home in real time, where the play of rational thought is always coming unmade, a world away from the taut drama of well-made play.

[1983]

The Real Life
of
Maria Irene Fornes

EVER SINCE *FEFU AND HER FRIENDS* MARIA IRENE FORNES HAS been writing the finest realistic plays in this country. In fact, one could say that *Fefu* and the plays that followed it, such as *The Danube* and now *Mud*, have paved the way for a new language of dramatic realism, and a way of directing it. What Fornes, as writer and director of her work, has done is to strip away the self-conscious objectivity, narrative weight, and behaviorism of the genre to concentrate on the unique subjectivity of characters for whom talking is gestural, a way of being. There is no attempt to tell the whole story of a life, only to distill its essence. Fornes brings a much needed intimacy to drama, and her economy of approach suggests another vision of theatricality, more stylized for its lack of exhibitionism. In this new theatricality, presence, that is, the act of being, is of greatest importance. The theatrical idea of presence is an aspect of the idea of *social being* expressed by character. The approach is that of a documentary starkness profoundly linked to existential phenomenology.

Fornes's work goes to the core of character. Instead of the usual situation in which a character uses dialogue or action to explain what he or she is doing and why, her characters exist in the world by their very act of trying to understand it. In other words, it is the characters themselves who appear to be thinking, not the author having thought.

Mud, which has as its center the act of a woman coming to thought, clarifies this process. Here is a poor rural trio, Fornes's first lower depths characters, which consists of Mae, Lloyd and Henry, all who lead lives devoid of any sense of play or abandonment; their lives are entirely functional. Each of them exists in varying relations to language—Mae through her desire to read and acquire knowledge realizes that knowledge is the beginning of will and power and personal freedom; Henry, who becomes crippled in an accident during the course of the play, must learn again how to speak; Lloyd, barely past the level of survival beyond base instincts, has no language of communication beyond an informational one. *Mud* is the encounter of the characters in seventeen scenes which are separated by slow blackouts of "eight seconds," the story of struggles for power in which Henry usurps Lloyd's place in Mae's bed, and Lloyd kills Mae when she eventually walks out on Henry and him and their destitute existence. The violence committed in this play is the violence of the inarticulate.

Through the plays of Bond, Kroetz, Fassbinder, Wenzel, Vinaver, to name a few, a new and different realism stripped bare, plays that outline the contemporary vision of tragedy, came into drama in the seventies in Europe. But this refinement of realism, to the extent that it could be called a movement, never happened here, largely because of the heavy input of psychology and speech in American theatre, the scant interest in stylized gesture and emotion, the lack of attention to the nuances of language as a political condition. (Though one could point to such plays as Tavel's *Boy on the Straight-Back Chair*, Shepard's *Action*, Mamet's *Edmond*, Shank's *Sunset/Sunrise* as steps toward an American rethinking of realism, they are only isolated phenomena.) What Fornes has done in her approach to realism over the years, and *Mud* is the most austere example of this style to be produced in the theatre on this side of the Atlantic, is to lift the burden of psychology, declamation, morality, and sentimentality from the concept of character. She has freed characters from explaining themselves in a way that attempts to suggest interpretations of their actions, and put them in scenes that create a single emotive moment, as precise in what it does not articulate as in what does get said.

She rejects bourgeois realism's clichés of thought patterns, how its characters project themselves in society; she rejects its melodramatic self-righteousness. Though her work is purposely presented in a flat space that emphasizes its frontality, and the actors speak in a non-inflected manner, it is not the detached cool of hyper- or super- or photo-realism, but more emotive, filled with content. Gestures, emptied of their excesses, are free to be more resonant. *The Danube* resounds with the unspeakable horror of nuclear death precisely because it is not named.

Mud's scenes seem, radically, to be a comment on what does not occur in performance, as if all the action had happened off stage. Her realism subtracts information whereas the conventional kind does little more than add it to a scene. She turns realism upside down by attacking its materialism and in its place emphasizing the interior lives of her characters, not their exterior selves. Hers is not a drama infatuated with things, but the qualities that make a life. Even when Henry buys Mae lipstick and a mirror in which to see herself, the moment is not for her a cosmetic action but a recognition of a self in the act of knowing, an objectification, a critique of the self.

There is no waste in this production. Fornes has always had a common sense approach to drama that situates itself in the utter simplicity of her dialogue. She writes sentences, not paragraphs. Her language is a model of direct address, it has the modesty of a writer for whom English is a learned language. She is unique in the way she writes about sexuality, in a tender way that accents sexual feelings, not sex as an event. It is a bitterly sad moment when Henry, his body twisted, his speech thick with pain, begs Mae to make love to him: "I feel the same desires. I feel the same needs. I have not changed." Emotion is unhidden in her plays. Just as language is not wasted, so the actors don't waste movements. Each scene is a strong pictorial unit. Sometimes a scene is only an image, or a few lines of dialogue. Here realism is quotational, theatre in close-up, freeze frame, theatre made by a miniaturist: in *The Danube* an acted scene is replayed in front of the stage by puppets, creating a fierce honorableness in its comment on human action. It is not imperialistic in its desire to create a world on a stage invested with moral imperatives, it is interested only in tableaux from a few lives in a particular place and time. Each scene presents a glimpse of imagery that is socially meaningful.

The pictorial aspect of this realism signifies an important change in theatrical attitudes towards space. Whereas traditional realism concerned itself with a confined physicality determined by "setting," the new realism is more open cosmologically, its characters iconic. That is one of the reasons why this emotive, aggressive realism is rooted in expressionist style. (Expressionism keeps realism from becoming melodrama.) Contemporary painting also turned to expressionism, after a period of super-realism, in order to generate an approach to emotion, narration and content. If styles change according to new perceptions of human form and its socialization, then painting and theatre, arts that must continually revise their opinions of figuration, should follow similar directions in any given period. Today, the exaggerated theatricality in everyday life has brought painting and theatre closer together.

The new realism would be confined by mere setting, which is only informational, it needs to be situated in the wider poetic notion of "space" which has ontological references. In the ecology of theatre, setting is a closed system of motion while space is more aligned to the idea of landscape which influences theatre, not only in writing but in design, as a result of now regarding the stage as "performance space." The very idea of space itself indicates how much the belief that all the world's a stage has been literalized. The concept of theatrical space alludes to the global repercussions of human action, if only metaphorically. (It is not coincidental that the concept of "performance space" developed in the same period, the sixties, as the exploration of outer space.)

In recent years Fornes has become such a self-assured director that the movement in her productions seems nearly effortless, totally inhibiting actorly artificiality. She doesn't force her actors' bodies on us in an attempt for them to dominate space. She leaves spaces on the stage unused. She makes the actors appreciate stillness as a theatrical idea, they are considerate toward other theatrical lives. And Fornes acknowledges the audience by giving them their own space and time in the productions. In *Mud* the short scenes and blackouts emphasize this attitude toward reception. They leave room for the audience to enter for contemplative moments. The authorial voice does not demand power over the theatrical experience. It is not territorial. There is room for subjectivity, as a corrective to evasive objectification, on the part of all those involved in the making and witnessing of the event. *Fefu and Her Friends* is the play that most literally invites the audience into the playing space—there were five of them to be exact—and for this Fornes created a style of acting that seemed, simply, a way of talking, it was so real.

Fornes has found her own stage language, a method of discourse that unites play, actor and space in an organic whole that is always showing how it thinks, even as it allows for fragments of thought, unruly contradictions. One of the characteristics of Fornes's plays is that they offer characters *in the process of thought*. Her characters often question received ideas, conventions, the idea of emotion, even how one engages in thought. "What would be the use of knowing things if they don't serve you, if they don't help you shape your life?" asks Mae, an only partially literate woman who yet is dignified with a mind, however limited in its reach. All thought must be useful to characters and find meaning through life itself, to allow life its fullest expression. *Mud* is imbued with a feminism of the most subtle order, feminism based on the ruling idea that a free woman is one who has autonomy of thought. So, it does not matter to the play that Mae is murdered because the main point has already been made: Mae is free because she can understand the concept of freedom.

On one level, Fornes's plays equate the pleasure of thinking with the measure of being. That so many of her plays, *Dr. Kheal, Tango Palace, Evelyn Brown,* besides those already mentioned here, to one degree or another deal with the acquisition of language, alludes to what must surely be one of her consistent interests: the relationship of language to thought to action. The dramatic language is finely honed to exclude excessive qualifiers, adjectives, clauses. Sentences are simple, they exist to communicate, to question. There is a purity to this language of understatement that does not assume anything, and whose dramatic potential rests in the search for meaning in human endeavor. That is why the human voice, as an embodiment of social values, has so significant a place in this kind of writing.

Fornes's work has a warm delicacy and grace that distinguish it from most of what is written today. Apart from her plays there is little loveliness in the theatre. And yet I must stop to include Joseph Chaikin and Meredith Monk in this special group of artists for they also reflect this "loveliness" of presence. Loveliness?—a humanism that guilelessly breathes great dignity into the human beings they imagine into life, and so propose to reality. Working for more than twenty years in off-Broadway's unheralded spaces, Fornes is an exemplary artist who through her writing and teaching has created a life in the theatre away from the crass hype that attends so many lesser beings. How has she managed that rare accomplishment in this country's theatre—a career? What is admirable about Fornes is that she is one of the last of the real bohemians among the writers who came to prominence in the sixties. She never changed to fit her style to fashion. She has simply been busy writing, working. If there were a dozen writers in our theatre with Fornes's wisdom and graciousness it would be enough for a country, and yet even one of her is, sometimes, all that is necessary to feel the worth of the enormous effort it takes to live a life in the American theatre.

[1984]

from

The Theatre of Images

The Theatre of Images
An Introduction

IN THE LAST DOZEN YEARS THE AMERICAN AVANT-GARDE theatre has emerged as a dynamic voice in the international arts scene. From its crude beginnings in out-of-the-way lofts, churches, private clubs and renovated spaces, it has become for many the liveliest, most creative center of theatrical activity in the West. This is due partly to the help of grant monies, but primarily to the emergence of a number of highly imaginative and gifted theatre artists.

Experimental groups of the sixties and early seventies broke down traditional parameters of theatrical experience by introducing new approaches to acting, playwriting and the creation of theatrical environments; they reorganized audience and performing space relationships, and eliminated dialogue from drama. Collaborative creation became the rule.

Value came increasingly to be placed on performance with the result that the new theatre never became a literary theatre, but one dominated by images—visual and aural. This is the single most important feature of contemporary American theatre, and it is characteristic of the works of groups *and* playwrights. As early as eight years ago Richard Kostelanetz pointed out the non-literary character of the American theatre when he wrote in *The Theatre of Mixed Means*:

> . . . the new theatre contributes to the contemporary cultural revolt against the pre-dominance of the word; for it is definitely a theatre for a post-literate (which is not the same as illiterate) age . . .

If this theatre refused to believe in the supremacy of language as a critique of reality, it offered a multiplicity of images in its place. Kostelanetz's McLuhaneque statement clarifies the direction that the American theatre has steadily followed since the Happenings. It has now culminated in a Theatre of Images—the generic term I have chosen to define a particular style of the American avant-garde which is represented [in *The Theatre of Images*] by Richard Foreman (Ontological-Hysteric Theater), Robert Wilson (Byrd Hoffman School of Byrds) and Lee Breuer (Mabou Mines).

The works of Foreman, Wilson and Breuer represent the climactic point of a movement in the American avant-garde that extends from The Living Theatre, The Open Theater, The Performance Group, The Manhattan Project and The Iowa Theatre Lab, to the "show and tell" styles of political groups like El Teatro Campesino, The San Francisco Mime Troupe and The Bread and Puppet Theatre. (And it is continued in the current proliferation of art-performances.) Today it is demonstrated in the image-oriented Structuralist Workshop of Michael Kirby and in the works of younger artists: *Sakonnet Point* by Spalding Gray and Elizabeth LeCompte; the "spectacles" of Stuart Sherman. All of the productions and groups mentioned above exclude dialogue or use words minimally in favor of aural, visual and verbal imagery that calls for alternative modes of perception on the part of the audience. This break from a theatrical structure founded on dialogue marks a watershed in the history of American theatre, a *rite de passage*.

The intention of this Introduction is to demonstrate the significance of this Theatre of Images, its derivation from theatrical and non-theatrical sources, its distinctively American roots in the avant-garde, its embodiment of a certain contemporary sensibility and its impact on audiences.

This essay, which will first isolate characteristics of the Theatre of Images and then deal at length with the specific pieces published here, will perhaps suggest an attitude to bring to this theatre. Hopefully, it will also offer helpful, new tools of analysis—an alternative critical vocabulary—with which to view contemporary theatre.

The absence of dialogue leads to the predominance of the stage picture in the Theatre of Images. This voids all considerations of theatre as it is conventionally understood in terms of plot, character, setting, language and movement. Actors do not create "roles." They function instead as media through which the playwright expresses his ideas; they serve as icons and images. Text is merely a pretext—a scenario.

The texts as published here (less so in the case of *The Red Horse Animation* which offers a comic book as a textual alternative) remain incomplete documents of a theatre that must be seen to be understood; one cannot talk about the works of Foreman, Wilson and Breuer without talking about their productions. Attending a theatrical performance is always an experience apart from reading a dramatic text; but a playscript *does* generally stand on its own merits as a pleasurable experience, indicating what it is about and usually giving a clue as to how it is staged. Conversely, reading Wilson's *A Letter for Queen Victoria* can be frustrating for readers attuned to theme, character, story, genre and logical language structure. There is scarcely a clue to its presentation in a script composed of bits and pieces of overheard conversations, television and films. Similarly, in Foreman's work, which insists on demonstrating what the works say (in Wittgensteinian-styled language games), to read the text alone is to lose the sensual delight and intellectual exchange of his theatre. And *The Red Horse Animation* is not a play at all.

Just as the Happenings had no immediate theatrical antecedents, the Theatre of Images, though not quite so renegade, has developed aesthetically from numerous non-theatrical roots. This is not to say that this movement disregards theatrical practices of the past: it is the application of them that makes the difference. More directly, the avant-garde must use the past in order to create a dialogue with it.

Foreman's work shows the influence (and the radicalization) of Brechtian technique; Breuer has acknowledged his attempt to synthesize the acting theories of Stanislavsky, Brecht and Grotowski; the productions of Wilson descend from Wagner. However, in their work, spatial, temporal and linguistic concepts are non-theatrically conditioned. Extra-theatrical influences have had a more formative impact. Cagean aesthetics, new dance, popular cultural forms, painting, sculpture and the cinema are important forces that have shaped the Theatre of Images. It is also logical that America, a highly technological society dominated by aural and visual stimuli, should produce this kind of theatre created, almost exclusively, by a generation of artists who grew up with television and movies.

The proliferation of images, ideas and forms available to the artist in such a culture leads to a crisis in the artist's choice of creative materials, and in his relationship to the art object. It is not surprising, then, that all of the pieces collected here are metatheatrical: They are about the making of art. In *Pandering to the Masses: A Misrepresentation* Foreman speaks directly to the audience (on tape) concerning the "correct" interpretation of events *as they occur*. The actors relate the formal "Outline" of the production at intervals in *Red Horse*. The result is a high degree of focus on process. How one sees is as important as what one sees.

This focus on process—the producedness, or seams-showing quality of a work—is an attempt to make the audience more conscious of events in the theatre than they are accustomed to. It is the idea of *being there* in the theatre that is the impulse behind Foreman's emphasis on immediacy in the relationship of the audience to the theatrical event.

The importance given to consciousness in the Theatre of Images is also manifest in its use of individual psychologies: Foreman in his psychology of art; Wilson in his collaboration with Christopher Knowles, an autistic teenager whose personal psychology is used as creative material (not as psychology of the disturbed); and in Breuer's interest in motivational acting. In *Pandering*, life and theatre merge as Foreman incorporates his thoughts into the written text. In *Queen Victoria*, Wilson adapts, if only partially, autistic behavior as an alternative, positive mode of perceiving life. Through Breuer's use of interior monologue, the consciousness of the Horse is explored in *Red Horse*.

Each artist refrains from developing character in a predictable, narrative framework which would evoke conditioned patterns of intellectual and emotional response. Like all modernist experiments, which necessarily suggest a new way to perceive familiar objects and events, their works agitate for radical, alternative modes of perception.

In the Theatre of Images the painterly and sculptural qualities of performance are stressed, transforming this theatre into a spatially-dominated one activated by sense impressions, as opposed to a time-dominated one ruled by linear narrative. Like modern painting, the Theatre of Images is timeless (*Queen Victoria* could easily be expanded or contracted), abstract and presentational (in *Red Horse*, images are both abstract and anthropomorphic), often static (the principle of duration rules the work of Foreman and Wilson); frequently the stage picture is framed two-dimensionally (in *Pandering* the actors are often poised in frontal positions). Objects are dematerialized, functioning in their natural rhythmic context. The body of the actor is malleable and pictorial—like the three actors who form multiple images of an Arabian steed lying *on* the performing space (*Red Horse*). It is the flattening of the image (stage picture) that characterizes the Theatre of Images, just as it does modern painting.

If the acting is pictorial, it is also nonvirtuosic, an inheritance from the new dance which emphasizes natural movement. This is an aesthetic quality of the particular branch of the avant-garde dealt with here. What I wish to suggest is that the Theatre of Images in performance demonstrates a radical refunctioning of naturalism. It uses the performer's natural, individual movements as a starting point in production. Of the artists featured in this Introduction, Foreman is the most thoroughly naturalistic. He allows performers (untrained) a personal freedom of expression while at the same time making them appear highly stylized in slow-motion, speeded-up, noninflectional patterns of speech or movement. He also pays a great deal of attention to actual situation and detail and the factor of time. Foreman's work is stylized yet naturalistic as are Alain Resnais's *Last Year at Marienbad* and Marguerite Duras's *India Song*.

The naturalism of nontraditional theatre is a curious phenomenon but one worth paying attention to because of its prevalence and diversity; it is also quite a paradox to admit that the avant-garde, in 1976, is naturalistic. In addition to being characteristic of the scripts printed here, it has shown itself in the production of David Gaard's *The Marilyn Project* directed last year by Richard

Schechner, in Scott Burton's recent art-performance *Pair Behavior Tableaux*, as well as in Peter Handke's play without words, *My Foot My Tutor*. In these works there is a high degree of stylization by performers who "naturally" engage in an activity which is presented pictorially.

Perhaps that is why, in the Theatre of Images, tableau is so often the chief unit of composition. Tableau, in fact, has been a dominant structure in the work of twentieth-century innovators: the Cubists, Gertrude Stein, Bertolt Brecht, Jean-Luc Godard, Alain Robbe-Grillet, Philip Glass, to name a few. It is evident in the work of Foreman, Wilson and Breuer as well. Tableau has the multiple function of compelling the spectator to analyze its specific placement in the artistic framework, stopping time by throwing a scene into relief, expanding time and framing scenes. In *Pandering*, the tableaux function as objects in a cubist space, very often confusing perception by the intrusion of a single kinetic element. The cinematic "cuts" of *Red Horse* frequently focus the actors in close up; "frames" are duplicated in the actual comic book documentation of the performance.

The stillness of tableau sequences suspends time, causing the eye to focus on an image, and slows down the process of input. This increases the critical activity of the mind. For Foreman it represents the ideal moment to impart taped directives to the audience; it also regulates the dialectical interplay of word and image.

Neither time nor space are bound by conventional law. Time is slowed-down, speeded-up—experienced as duration. It is never clocked time. Likewise, spatial readjustment is frequent in all of the pieces discussed here. *Red Horse* is played in multiple viewing perspectives: the actors perform both lying on the floor and standing on it, and up against a back wall of the performing space. *Pandering* alternates easily from flat perspective to linear perspective; the actors continually rearrange the drapes and flats of the set during performance. In *Queen Victoria* space is divided, cut apart and blackened—usually by means of light—leaving the actors to serve as images or silhouettes in a surreal landscape.

If time and space are dysynchronous in the Theatre of Images, so is language broken apart and disordered. The language of *Queen Victoria* is "throwaway," devoid of content. In *Red Horse* choral narrative is correlated with the image in space as interior monologue substitutes for dialogue. *Pandering* is ruled by the distributive principle of sound: actors speak parts of sentences which are completed either by other actors or Foreman's voice on tape.

Sound is used sculpturally, just as the actors are. Aural tableaux complement or work dialectically with visual tableaux. In *Pandering* the audience, surrounded by stereo speakers, is bombarded with sound. Sound and visual images dominate in performance in an attempt to expand normal capabilities for experiencing sense stimuli. Because of the sophisticated sound equipment used in the productions of Foreman, Wilson and Breuer it is reasonable to conclude that the Theatre of Images would not exist without the benefit of advanced technology. Perhaps experiments with holography may lead in the future to a theatre of total images and recorded sound.

The significance of the Theatre of Images is its expansion of the audience's capacity to perceive. It is a theatre devoted to the creation of a new stage language, a visual grammar "written" in sophisticated perceptual codes. To break these codes is to enter the refined, sensual worlds this theatre offers. . . .

[1977]

The Ontological-Hysteric Theater
of
Richard Foreman

RICHARD FOREMAN IS A PHILOSOPHER-PLAYWRIGHT, AN ANOMaly in the American theatre which has never been a philosophical one. In his work with the Ontological-Hysteric Theater Foreman takes as his point of departure the philosophical, psychological and aesthetic writings of modern thinkers—in short, the Western epistemological tradition. Here is an avantgardist who is also a classicist. Foreman both challenges and respects the foundations of contemporary thought.

The Ontological-Hysteric Theater dramatizes thinking processes in a highly complex series of images. In *Pandering to the Masses: A Misrepresentation* Foreman creates a reality that reflects his own being-in-the-world, demonstrating in the process a rigorous, alternative manner of focusing on familiar, everyday events. *Pandering*, then, functions on two levels. The subjective nature of the play co-exists with the objective relationship of the audience to the theatre event (the central focus of the production).

Pandering appears, on the surface, to have dialogue. However, it is not dialogue as understood in usual theatre terms. In Foreman's conception of dramaturgy the spoken language is not only nondiscursive but flattened out through the elimination of inflectional patterns. This flatness is duplicated in the performances of the actors whose attention to detail and emphasis on natural rhythms of movement and speech produce an extreme naturalism. Speech is disconnected from the speaker by means of interruptive devices such as the tape-recorded Voice (of Foreman) and the voices of the other actors (live and on tape). Instead of engaging in conversational dialogue with one another, the actors, who function as "speakers," serve as the media of Foreman's ideas; they are "demonstrators."

The Ontological-Hysteric Theater is a theatre of illustrations in which pictures, continually interrelating with words, replace dialogue. Language exists in the domain of the phenomenological, used merely to indicate a reality in space; space becomes semantic. Foreman is Husserl's "meditating phenomenologist" who, in *Pandering*, meditates on his own and others' attitudes towards art.

In *Pandering* Foreman's focal point is the dual subject of the creation of art and the audience's perception of it. He challenges the popular notion of the acquisition of knowledge about an art object, in a dialectical framework that is highly personal.

In performance the actors function cubistically, as multiple facets of Foreman's personality, varying degrees of his subconscious. They also reflect his observations while writing *Pandering*. This accounts for the documentary aspect of the play which, on one level, is a record of Foreman's thoughts while he was in the actual process of creating the play.

The actors, then, serve as blank faces (negative physiognomies) on which Foreman sketches aspects of his "being-in-the-world"; they are representatives of figures of his inner life, playing out the contradictions of his life as a social being. The writer Max is the pivotal figure of the play; he embodies Foreman, the creative artist. Rhoda is the thematic representative of sexuality. Together they manifest the interplay of the intellectual and the sensual which dominates the play. In this display of first-person consciousness Foreman offers the purest form of psychodrama viewed up to this time in the American theatre. One scene, in particular, illustrates the personal factor of *Pandering*. Toward the end of the production a man on a bicycle peddles furiously (he represents the energy force of Knowledge) while firing shots at Rhoda. The Voice offers a word —"IKON"—to explain the psychological maneuver which follows this scene. Then, the Voice continues:

> He [Max] inhabits that word. That means to celebrate finally he thinks about his face as being her face so he thinks about his person as being her person finally, and worships it finally, and reads it finally like a wonderful book.

Rhoda is a substitute for Max who, in actuality, is Richard Foreman. Rhoda functions as both icon and idea.

On a second level, Foreman carries on a dialogue with the history of Western thought in which he attacks conventional modes of acquiring knowledge; in particular, knowledge gained in the perception of an event. *Pandering* is as much a play about Foreman as it is about the audience. In the staging of it Foreman sits in the first row of audience bleachers. From this vantage point he operates the tape system for the production (with himself as the taped Voice that dominates the work) while also identifying himself as an audience member by his presence among the spectators. From this dual perspective of author-spectator the Voice on tape comments on the kinds of responses elicited by the "old theatre." At one point in the production the Voice declares:

> The old theater would prove to you that Max is dancing the way that he is dancing, by which is meant, his motives, proven real and genuine, and you are convinced in a way appropriate to the theater.

Interestingly, *Pandering* bears a striking resemblance to Peter Handke's *Sprechstücke* which eliminate dramatic dialogue, employ "speakers" or "demonstrators" rather than characters, construct a dialogue between stage and audience, and debate with conventional theatre. Likewise, Foreman's work can be looked upon as "autonomous prologues to old plays" (Handke's phrase). And *Pandering to the Masses: A Misrepresentation* is as ironic a title as Handke's *Offending the Audience*—both are the "speak-ins" (*Sprechstücke*) of their authors.

Pandering is presented to the audience in the form of a "lecture-demonstration." Verbal and visual images accompany Foreman's running commentary. For example, the Voice remarks on the occasion of one of Rhoda's adventures:

> . . . every experience though perhaps peripheral to primary revelation of knowledge, friendship, and inventiveness, still every experience can be a learning experience if allowed to take its place in the mapping process of one's private adventure and spatial self orientation.

Projected slides ("legends"), which one may consider a more sophisticated variation of flash cards than those used by teachers in classrooms, carry content, which corresponds to or contradicts the image on stage, or describes an image that has already appeared or is about to appear ("He goes to the wall / finds two peepholes"). At the opening of the piece the Voice virtually insults the audience's intelligence in a "lecture" that declares:

> You understand nothing. Max regretfully concludes that you who watch and wait have unfortunately proven through your actions and reactions that certain subtle, exact, specific and necessary areas of understanding are not available to your—

The audience is left to fill in the blank.

Frequent "recapitulations" in the text reflect Foreman's didacticism. Yet they also have other functions. They serve as a flashback technique, or to further the action of the production by the interaction between Foreman and the actor on stage; often, they reinforce the memory of past events or clarify certain points of the text. In one instance, a "recapitulation" is calculated to make the audience reflect on the associative mode of perception. Foreman chides the audience, "Do you think using the associative method? Everybody does, you know." Like Gertrude Stein, whose writings, he has admitted, have been a major influence on his aesthetic theories, Foreman contrives to destroy associational emotion in the experience of a work of art. More significant, however, is Foreman's ability to create in his work what Stein referred to as the "actual present." *Pandering* exists in a dual framework: as the actual diary—the personal notes—of the playwright while he was writing the play over a certain period of time. The past and present merge in the actuality of the performance.

In another allusion to a major Steinian concern, the Voice directly confronts the issue of which image on stage takes precedence over another in the sequence of events:

> You can either watch Max writing it, or you can watch what he is writing. But you can only watch what he is writing after he is writing it, and in that case your expectations are in a different direction, are they not?

Similarly, in a lecture entitled "Plays" (1934) Gertrude Stein observed that the audience is always ahead of or behind a play on stage, never exactly "with it."

To both Stein and Foreman it is the *conscious* act of experiencing events at a certain time and place that is important. In *Pandering* Foreman seeks the triumph of the conscious over the unconscious.

Pandering is a consciousness-raising piece—a teaching play—whose goal is to make audience members aware of their moment-by-moment existence in the theatre. For this reason alienating devices obtrude throughout the production. Foreman continually breaks down the production into smaller and smaller units or frames. He imposes a play, *Fear*, within the play. Many of the actors' lines are prerecorded on tape in Foreman's Voice which interrupts them; the actors interrupt each other's speeches when each word in a sentence is spoken by a different person. Buzzers, loud thuds and music focused directionally by four stereo speakers which surround the audience, punctuate the actors' words. Scene titles, when they are used, break the flow of the production.

Foreman's use of these "alienation effects," more directly, his conception of a play as a "teaching play," reflects his Brechtianism. However, he is formalistically more radical than Brecht. Foreman breaks up his scenes into smaller and smaller units; Brecht divided his epic structures into unified scenic elements. Foreman is a minimalist concerned with instantaneous perception; Brecht's view was epic and historical, concerned not so much with momentary perception but with critical thinking which would lead to political activism outside the theatre. In Brecht's productions the actor "commented" on or "quoted" a past action; *Pandering* strives to create a continuous present even as it treats events of the past, i.e., Foreman's thoughts while writing it. Furthermore, though both artists devised dialectical theatres of illustration, Foreman has gone further than Brecht by moving the dialogue from its fixed position in a play on stage to a dialogue (metaphorical) between stage and audience. In this way, the dialectical aspect does not remain solely in the framework of the play on stage but occurs directly in the relationship of the audience to the production *in process*. (Handke has also accomplished this in his *Sprechstücke*.) Foreman always demonstrates *how* the play works.

Pandering emphasizes its producedness, i.e., the interconnection of its parts. This focus on structure necessarily compels the audience to scan it for minute alterations. By calling attention to itself—how it works—it stimulates the audience's powers of perception. The Ontological-Hysteric Theater is radically opposed to the traditional theatre (what Brecht called the "culinary" theatre) which feeds information to the audience by suggesting the "proper" emotions and responses to stage events. In Foreman's theatre there are no touchstones, no recognizable pegs on which to hang conditioned responses or ideas. The world of the play, while not duplicating reality, suggests a way to view life in the real world. Through Foreman's reduction of his personal life to a series of images one is led to perceive things as they are in themselves—not by learned patterns of perception but in an unconditioned way. Observation supersedes memory.

Foreman's emphasis on change, conscious response, the present moment, his use of "recapitulation" and taped directives for viewing *Pandering* force the audience to be aware of the making-of-theatre. Thus, the process of *Pandering* is always evident. During performance the actors virtually construct the set of the play, redistribute space (expanding, contracting, deepening it) by means of props, sliding frames and drapes. The actors themselves are sometimes "constructed." Fitted at times with objects and cloth, they appear like assemblage art. In one scene dolls are strapped to the legs of the actresses for a musical number.

In the world of *Pandering*, where gesture is dissociated from language or merges with it, where language is fragmented and thought dislocated, time is experienced in terms of changing spatial relationships. In the design of the set Foreman plays purposefully with perspective: a road leading to a house at the back of the playing area narrows to its end ("Try looking through the wrong end of the telescope. Everything looks sharper, doesn't it?" asks the inquisitive Voice). Many scenes are presented in slow motion, suggesting a two-dimensional, painterly perspective. The actors frequently stare at the audience or gaze sideways; other scenes are presented from the perspective of the picture-frame stage. The continual rearticulation of space which Foreman's long and deep but narrow loft theatre affords, complicates perception of movement and disorients the audience which must accordingly change its field of vision to accommodate the variety of spatial configurations.

Foreman's idiosyncratic use of strings, which dangle from the ceiling and stretch in horizontal rows or diagonal crosses about the performing space, sectionalizes space and cuts it into geometric shapes. Another use of the strings has more to do with Foreman's insistent directorial focus on elements within the stage picture: his pointing out certain correspondences between the words and the images. When a performer, for example, draws a string from one end of the space to another until it touches a person or object, that person or object is defined in an exact point of time and space, as well as in reference to other activities on stage. In this way the world of *Pandering* presents a diagrammatic reality whose system of reference is entirely within the play as performed. Foreman's work is conceptual art, i.e., self-defining.

The rhythmic element of the piece is carried from unit to unit. The sound of a metronome during the production articulates its beats, affirming the musicality of the work. Foreman's work in the theatre parallels the trance or minimal music of such diverse composers as Philip Glass, LaMonte Young, Terry Riley and Steve Reich in whose compositions the accretion of sound is a key structural feature. Glass, in particular, has written:

> . . . nothing happens in the usual sense . . . instead, the gradual accretion of musical material can and does serve as the basis of the listener's attention . . . neither memory nor anticipation . . . have a place in sustaining the texture, quality or reality of the musical experience.

His statement, from a program note for a 1973 Town Hall concert, accurately describes the ambience of *Pandering*, which is constructed from the gradual build-up of small units of composition.

Conversely, subtraction—pause or silence—is important to *Pandering* as an interruptive device and a way of slowing down the performance, as is playing the taped Voice against the natural voices of the actors by subtracting them from their words. John Cage was the first to regard silence as a viable structural unit of music, overthrowing much of traditional compositional theory which had viewed time in music as an empty unit to be filled. In the dance world Yvonne Rainer and others of the Judson Dance Theatre and post-Judson period experimented with time as duration and the subtraction of movement. They were often joined by artists such as Robert Rauschenberg and Robert Morris who worked very specifically with new concepts of movement through time and the placement of objects in space. Foreman has solid foundations in post-Cagean aesthetics as they have filtered through the worlds of art, music and dance. His exploration of movement and spatial organization, elasticization of time, and radical situation of objects in the construction of his productions have been, and still are, dominant preoccupations of New York avant-garde artists.

Foreman's application of silence is significantly demonstrated in his use of tableau—the subtraction of the moving image. Tableau is *Pandering*'s chief unit of composition, a still life which frames the action and "quotes" it. This quoting of gesture is another Brechtian technique that finds expression in Foreman's theatre; however, Foreman's employment of tableau, because it occurs more frequently and lasts longer than Brechtian tableau, elasticizes time as well as continually disrupting the spatial flow of the production. In tableau Foreman's actors appear as frozen voids in space—like the chalk-white faceless forms in a Chirico landscape—until they are revived by the tape machine or a change of scenery.

Tableau is used in various ways: the duplication of gestures in foreground and background; close-up perspective; the inclusion of a single kinetic element in an otherwise frozen picture; a confrontation of the audience vis-à-vis the actors in a frontal position; and for iconographic effect. Finally, by employing tableaux which throw certain elements of the production into high relief, Foreman is able to bracket perception of events on stage, thereby drawing attention to particular elements of the stage picture.

The framing of events on stage is paralleled by the framing of objects in which a single element is presented in close-up against a larger, more complicated background of activity. For instance, in the palm of his hand an actor in a foreground position holds a letter in an envelope which is affixed to a plate: it is another way in which Foreman breaks the continuity of composition by extreme reduction of a scene or gesture. Windows, boxes and cutouts in the design of the set frame objects or people, such as Rhoda's breasts exhibited in a door frame.

Curiously, Foreman's published notes and manifestoes reiterate his fascination with framing. Sentences are often subdivided by parentheses, brackets and equation symbols; rather than flowing smoothly they focus on single elements.

The framing devices and tableaux of *Pandering*, in addition to disrupting the flow of time, draw attention to its passage. Time exists, as it were, in the continuous present of the dream world where images of the subconscious appear, drift away and then reappear, or collide with other images. Space repeatedly changes its contours in defiance of physical laws so that a wall of a room gives way to a jungle and scenes shift easily from outdoors to indoors. The people who inhabit this surreal world are free to roam with abandon through a series of adventures that take them back and forth in time and place. It is the landscape of Foreman's mind, the image-activated visions of his subconscious. Scattered about in this world are fruit, an oversized horse and giant pencils, croquet balls, stuffed animals, a pistol, a snake and bicycle—all of which have symbolic value in Foreman's psychodrama. These are the symbols of childhood, of violence, of power and fear, temptation and sensuality.

In his situation of objects and people in *Pandering* Foreman recalls similar styles of the personal, surrealist films of Jean Cocteau and the American experimentalist Maya Deren. Foreman shares with them his love of melodrama, eroticism of violence, the placement of the human figure against a plane, narcissism, and the distortion of time and space through the use of mirrors and walls. However, Foreman's work differs from their classical surrealism in its demand for rigorous control rather than spontaneous expression, the importance given to phenomenological activity, and its high degree of cerebralism. Seen in another light, Foreman's filmic inheritance may be what P. Adams Sitney, in his book, *Visionary Film: The American Avant-Garde*, observed as the American avant-garde cinema's unacknowledged aspiration: "the cinematic reproduction of the human mind." *Pandering to the Masses: A Misrepresentation* is a *theatrical* reproduction of the human mind—Richard Foreman's. He creates in his theatre a new way of thinking about the theatre event, a greater consciousness of art. Not only does he make theatre going more meaningful, but life as well.

[1977]

Performances

Essaying Images
The Archaeology of Consciousness
Meredith Monk's *Recent Ruins*

beginning again

For the overture the singers sit in a "magic" circle that is the consecrated space from which their incantation calls up the spirits of the past. Is *Recent Ruins* the dream of these people who revisit their primitive past and envision their future?

The solo and choral singing (female voices dominate) is of a pre-verbal order that is a kind of poetry, but it is the *body* of the voice that attracts attention. In this dance opera (there is no spoken language) it is the landscape of the body that reflects its geography of dreams. The singing is not the "beautiful" kind that hides all the work and shows only the refined surfaces, but "crude" singing that incorporates the journey theme of the piece by showing how sound travels in and through the body. Sometimes you can hear it curling up and over the teeth, in the nose, the back of the throat, and in the diaphragm.

Certain letters of the alphabet are prominent—"w," "a," "o"—the non-aggressive, soft sounds, and the singing sometimes incorporates talking, as if language is on the way to becoming. The sounds are birth cries, animal noises, screams, lullabies—undifferentiated sound in a universe that does not yet have names for things.

It is primal sound whose dominant quality is the echo: as if these tones always existed and will always exist in space. Musical motifs of the overture will re-echo in other sections of the work, starting as the acoustic sound of earliest life and ending as recorded sound after the world moves from primitive to technological society.

The phenomenology of sound is conceptualized musically to define a world in which all harsh sounds are excluded and only those (w, o, m, b, a) which take in and give out the life breath find a space.

writing a performance

Section II. While the twentieth-century couple sits on the upper stage in front of a projection screen behind which someone is drawing examples of ancient and modern artifacts, pairs of "archaeologists" write equations and calculations all over the floor. When this segment concludes, a film made by Monk at Ellis Island details the classification and documentation of immigrants on a screen directly across the space from the position of the couple.

This section of *Recent Ruins* represents the modern obsession, begun in the Renaissance, with codifying and documenting everything in the world: the world is viewed in terms of its Objecthood. The performance text itself is *written* in theatrical time, not only literally, but in narrative codes that are spatial, acoustic, iconographic, chromatic, diagrammatic, kinesic, symbolic. The huge anonymous hand (reminding us that these objects were first *handi*crafts, later industrial objects) draws a "lesson": that objects, like people, have a history. The "language" of the humanistic perspective is written on the floor, on the screen, on the film frame (an immigrant's nose is circled as a hand writes "Serb" across the film strip).

This then is the culmination of the humanist view Galileo summed up in his dream "to measure everything measurable and to make what is not measurable capable of being measured." Monk's repertory of images exposes a geometry of emotion in which the materialism of humanism is displaced by the dematerialist world spirit she proposes.

the portrait and the tableau

The portrait is a compositional unit of *Recent Ruins*. In this particular instance it is a play on images that contrasts the real and the cinematic images of the immigrants who appear live (here) at first, then shortly thereafter in a film.

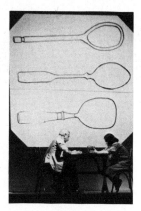

On the ground in front of them is a jug like the one in the projected drawings alongside the table of the couple in the "domestic tableau" (the immigrants and the couple dominate opposite ends of the space). From left to right, a woman alone, weary and fearful; a black man, situated slightly behind the women, withdrawn, skeptical; a wide-eyed, hopeful woman bringing a baby to the "new world."

The portrait represents an attitude toward history, it puts history in quotes. Unlike the *tableau* which is interested in imagery, a *portrait* is rooted in social commentary. The tableau is only understood in the context of the work as a whole; the portrait lives in its own world.

a change of perspective

Everytime I look at these two "archaeologists" (section II) in Victorian dress roaming about, measuring, and making calculations in chalk on the floor, I think of Gertrude Stein and Alice B. Toklas who undertook many amateur archaeological expeditions in the European countryside. (A generous theatre experience always allows the spectator some time to dream.)

Stein's intellectual excavation of the visible and invisible in the world led her to conceive of a work of art as a "landscape"—it would reflect everything in it in a state of continuous present. "The only thing that is different from one time to another is what is seen and what is seen depends upon how everybody is doing everything," she once said in another context.

digression #1

When Susan Sontag published her provocative essay, "Against Interpretation," in 1964 she probably didn't suspect the impact it would have on art and literary worlds. Nor, I'm sure, would she agree with the ways in which her articulate, forceful polemic would be pushed to extremes by those seeking to proclaim the objectivity of aesthetic experience.

One must see that essay in its historical context as Sontag herself emphasized in it more than once, referring to its context "today"—that was sixteen years ago. Her essay took a position against the kind of criticism that was devoted to the moral view in a work of art, and the psychology (Freudian) it reflected, written by critics bent on a search for meaning in sub-texts of their own creation. The sensuality of a work of art was undermined by the obsession to wring content from form.

Though several significant changes have occurred which invite one to re-examine Sontag's early position, there are two that have special relevance in the contemporary context: the success of conceptual art which trivialized the division of form and content; the influence of structuralism which radicalized the ways it is possible to think about a text.

Sontag, however, had already left the way open for the act of interpretation in the right circumstances. "It is reactionary, impertinent, cowardly, stifling," she said, but also allowed that "in some cultural contexts, interpretation is a liberating act."

I believe that today provides the cultural context for making interpretation a liberating act, but I am concerned with the idea of interpretation only in the context of performance (avant-garde performance, to be specific) which in the last dozen years has radically extended the variety of theatrical experience. Performance, which by its nature devises an image language, invites criticism that can be sensually involved with the structure of images in complex ways, while not reducing everything to content. That doesn't mean that discussion of a performance need begin and end with the point of empathy of the spectator interpreting the psychology of the performer or author.

The writings of Paul Ricoeur suggest a way to revitalize Sontag's essay vis-à-vis avant-garde performance which has gone beyond sophisticated formal experimentation while critics lag far behind, lacking the vocabulary to address performance, and so resorting most often to mere description of the event.

The subject of interpretation has special relevance with regard to theatrical presentation because theatre is a shared event (unlike the isolated reading of a literary text) that takes place publicly, and is always in the *state of becoming.* Theatrical performances can never be reinterpreted years or generations after they occur, which means that performance criticism always begins on the experiential plane, and is always sensually involved.

Ricoeur sees the world as "an ensemble of references opened up by texts." He moves the emphasis of interpretation away from the study of the author and toward the understanding of the *world* of his work. In Ricoeur's view the meaning of a text is not behind it (the place where Sontag finds mediocre interpreters excavating for meaning) but in front of it, to be disclosed by the text itself. It is the difference between seeking and finding.

If in pre-structuralist times (in America, that is) Sontag wanted to keep the reader from re-writing, so to speak, a work of art, now that structuralism has re-imagined the relationship of text and reader, Ricoeur can suggest that work is written again in the reader who expands his capacity for knowing himself by understanding in the world of the work new modes of being-in-the-world. Thus, the big leap is moving the act of interpretation away from the subjective plane on to the ontological one.

It is at this point that we can begin to think of a hermeneutics of performance which can show us that all the stage is a world.

the theatre of images

Recent Ruins is pure performance text opening up to a field of energies whose every sound and image is lexicalized into signs that evolve a semantic space. The performance text—in this way it is like a literary text—is capable of carrying on a sophisticated narrative discourse, but it proposes a sensual grammar in lieu of a linguistic one: one of movement (kinesics), one of images (iconology), one of sound (oral poetry).

If imagery in contemporary performance has frequently become seductive, solipsistic, and empty of extended cultural metaphor, *Recent Ruins* proves an exception by affirming the ideational impact of imagery when constituted in radical cultural contexts. We need a kind of performance criticism that moves beyond the description of imagery to a hermeneutics of imagery.

Throughout its brief history the American avant-garde has conceived poetically complex relationships between text and image, but in very few cases has it discarded language altogether in favor of imagery. Monk has succeeded, as has Robert Wilson, in creating a pure theatre of images because she deals with myth, archetypes and consciousness as subject matter. Her imagery lives in the idea of culture and its psychology reflects, not the self of autobiographical art, but the soul of mythopoesis. Her structures of images embody a formal integrity that is always on the verge of becoming allegory.

Ellis Island is a recent ruin where human beings were once segregated, examined, measured, and classified like artifacts of history. The island itself symbolized an isolated universe that cut off the immigrant from the home land, the community, ritual experience, and the mother tongue. It demonstrated it wasn't true that "no man is an island." Pre-industrial realities of experience were displaced by industrial, then technological fantasies of Progress which is the idea that made it possible to accept the transformation of huge sections of the American landscape into recent

ruins. In most parts of the world ruins put one in the state of mind to reflect on history while our ruins deny the role of history in American life.

In the ethnographic collections of any museum one can always overhear visitors commenting on the "modernity" of ancient artifacts. "Look how modern those bracelets (bowls, tools) are." They never acknowledge that industry merely continues the structural features and uses of ancient objects. All objects in bourgeois consumer society have to be looked upon as if they never existed before so that people will always have the feeling that they own something brand new.

the pictorial and the imagistic

The pictorial is a representation of an action whose predictability and shape is never in question; it is illustrative. Imagery is always a surprise because it springs from Necessity, not causality. Pictures are merely anecdotal, decorative; images are poetic, mythic. The old theatre is literal, the new theatre is metaphoric. Now imagery and imagination can begin to create the morality of form.

the semiotics of space

When I think of affecting theatrical experiences of recent years, besides *Recent Ruins* the two that come immediately to mind are *Quarry* (also Monk) and the Greek Trilogy of Andrei Serban, all three of them presented, coincidentally, in the performing space of La Mama Annex. That space is a horizontal space which is the ideal setting for myth and ritual presentation. In the Oriental theatre it is the model of the cosmos.

Recent Ruins has its upper and lower regions, corners, center, light and dark areas where simultaneous action in different settings can represent in non-linear sequence all time, dramatic time, filmic time, musical time. If the experience of verticality is modernist, horizontal space is timeless, spiritual. It is the space where history can confront the audience today.

The ideas of history are conceptualized in the use of space as historical setting: flat, simple space for the primitive scene (section III); stereometric space as the modern experience (section II); sensual, conceptualized imagery-as-narration in the new vision that projects itself into the future (section IV).

an anthropological note: That women choreographers (Monk, Trisha Brown, Kei Takei come immediately to mind) use the floor as setting more so than men, suggests an historical link with women at the (h)earth.

This is part of a sequence in which two figures move from a simian to a human state. Monk's interpretation of the first encounter of man and woman before the Fall shows them as equal partners in their relationship. The woman is not shown to be the corruptor.

digression #2

How should a feminist critique of *Recent Ruins* proceed? Should the work be explained by the fact that Monk is a woman or should it be explained by her position as choreographer, or does her humanist vision dominate the creation? I resist seeing a work of art in terms of any system other than the one it creates for itself, yet it would be unfair to deny that certain ways of thinking about human life have been expanded by the feminist perspective (as they have by Marxism), and that this work is one of them.

Monk's work cannot be totally explained from the point of view of its woman-centeredness, yet it is important to see in it an alternative to received (i.e., male) perceptions of the historical process, and an acknowledgement of women's contribution to culture and the repository of myth, before making the jump to understanding the non-sexually differentiated model of consciousness it presents as its unifying idea. If theatre has any function it has to be to shape new models of consciousness in a living situation. In the feminist context it simply means shifting the perspective of women from object to subject.

Monk re-visions history by acknowledging the myth of heroic women in ancient times: the woman warrior leading the community and the goddess defending herself from human transgressions.

Section III depicts a matriarchal society (in the primitive culture segments the performers wear yellow) whose members dance and sing with joy after one of them has subdued the giant goddess. They dance in pure ritual pleasure—a dance that is uninhibited, outward-directed, individualistic, heavenward—around the magic waters (the circle of the prologue) wherein the universal eye is reflected.

The male and female (they dominate) voices, in typically tribal call and response pattern answer "oo-oo" to the melody line of "a-we-na" that is chanted over and over. In the thematic context of *Recent*

Ruins Gaston Bachelard's observation has special meaning as a poetics of space. ". . . the vowel *a* is the vowel of immensity. It is a sound that starts with a sigh and extends beyond all limits."

the archaeology of consciousness

I

One recent afternoon I was walking with a director friend who remarked at the sight of a gray, filmy vapor in the sky above us: "Are they dropping the bomb before I finish my piece on nuclear power?" Later that evening an unprepossessing helicopter hovered overhead, and some passersby looked up with fear on their faces. What do these incidents suggest?—that the real threat of nuclear holocaust has entered our consciousness, reconstituting the myth of the Apocalypse.

II

Once upon a time in the sixties ritual, the ideals of communitas, and the study of myth influenced the radical narrative strategies of artists who attempted to understand consciousness. Then, myth came to mean personal mythology. The threat of war will move theatre people away from self-centered art and toward chronicling the life of the community. The solo voice will be displaced by the group chant once again.

III

Recent Ruins opposes the notion of what some critics and scholars call "schizo-culture"—the history of the individual viewed in relation to his fragmentation and contradictions (Richard Foreman and Spalding Gray represent this position)—by affirming instead the wholeness of the individual at home in a world that reflects unity and continuity. In place of dialectics between split selves Monk proposes a more holistic view of the human organism.

The world of *Recent Ruins* outlines an historical view of human consciousness in three phases:

> primitive society; the modern, humanist vision that began in the Renaissance; the cosmic consciousness that is beginning to be thought of today as post-humanism.

Reinforcing the archaeological metaphor is the sand and stone that fall from the ceiling above the performance space at the end of each historical section as if, phenomenologically speaking, to force one temporarily to bracket existence.

the future as history

The final image unites human beings and nature, myth and technology, earth and sky in a non-hierarchical vision of a cosmic whole. Monk's new spiritual topography doesn't presuppose the creation of a new human form so much as it situates the history of human life in a new equation with the cosmos.

The algebra of the intellectual position is symbolized in the iconography of the last tableau which shows human figures surrounded by familiar (if giant) phenomena—turtles which remind them of the possibility of longevity, a spider (held by the goddess of section III) whose web emphasizes the cycles of life and bees (not seen in photograph), the industrious, creative forces of life. In the darkness people in black (the piece opens and closes in black and white—the shades of infinity) twirl small models of satellites which expand the possibilities of global communication and bring us closer to life in space.

The miniaturization of the satellites and the enlargement of animal life reverse the natural representations of the visible world, and in this act of the imagination we can glimpse poetically Monk's visionary world which is not in the future, it's already here.

[1980]

Music Performance
A Few Notes

1   Throughout this century the live presentation of vocal music has followed two distinct, and opposite, traditions: one is the approach to *performing* a song, the other to *singing* a song. In the distinction I am proposing, a song performed shapes an attitude toward the song lyrics that clearly defines the performer's point of view *as a social being*: the tone of voice, humor, audience-performer relationship, and body gestures signal the presence of an active, thinking mind in the musical action, beyond the matter of skillful presentation.

Performing a song differs from the romantic tradition of singing which claims singers such as Frank Sinatra, Tony Bennett, Sarah Vaughan, Judy Garland, Lena Horne, to name a few, and also from the more formalistic approaches of Mel Torme, Peggy Lee, and Cleo Laine who put so much of themselves technically into a song that at times they seem outside of it—but only emotionally, not socially. In each case an *individual* musical identity dominates the lyrical phrase. The "singer" emphasizes each unit of the song for its own sake, identifying with the emotional moments it evokes, in an attempt to recreate that moment in the audience.

Those whose styles suggest what I mean by "performance," and who include artists as diverse as David Bowie, Bette Midler, Peter Allen, Meredith Monk, Robert Wilson, Laurie Anderson, Philip Glass and Robert Ashley bring a politicized thinking, even a dimension of myth, to song which links the audience and them, *anthropologically*, to a particular moment in a shared cultural history. In terms of audience reception this is not the same experience as embracing a song as an individual moved by a private emotional moment in a public setting. "Singing," which elicits that response, doesn't separate the singer from the song, so there is no exchange in the aesthetic space between the two, except when the private life of the singer intrudes on the public one, and the audience begins to read autobiographical fact in the fictional lines of a song—Garland and Edith Piaf were particularly vulnerable in this situation, and it was part of their great appeal to audiences. (The same blurred "realities" can occur between an actor and a role.)

2 As a way of making music, *performance* outlines the iconoclastic, vanguard impulse toward song in its refusal simply to illustrate the images of a song text, instead generating its own in relation to the song—this counter imagery can be aural, it can be visual (situated in the stance of the performer), it can be sociological. It is always anti-illusionistic. In any case, it is a *theatrical* idea about singing (rather than a psychological one) that works itself out in relation to a live audience encouraged to participate in a communal act of social consciousness.

Performing a song is to singing a song what performance is to acting (one style is self-conscious, presentational; the other is representational, character-oriented). It involves commenting on the substance of a text rather than inhabiting it uncritically or merely acting it out, but more important, this attitude relates the song to the world beyond the lyrics, to that very world inhabited by the audience. The relationship of performance to song is shown in the way that the performer makes the song work on several levels—significantly, these two: the first, a kind of theatrical aside to the audience, the second a dialogue between performer and song. (A solo performer has more direct, personal freedom in this dialogue than one who performs in a musical play, but the seeming restriction of a narrative opens up many more narrative possibilities of communication belonging to the world of theatre.) Performance adds a new dimension to the idea of *presence* on stage, enlarging the definition beyond that of charisma, to include historical consciousness, the fleshiness of being overtaking elusive spirit.

Not coincidentally, in the world of theatre this idea reached its most brilliant form in the collaboration of Brecht and Weill who made the *performed* song the basis of their political aesthetics. The theatre they created was situated in the idea of a *social* relationship between performer and song, between the song and the broader text of the play, and between the world of the play and the social reality outside of it. All of the single theatrical elements worked together dialectically, in relationships that turned on irony, a self-conscious attitude by nature dependent on an audience for its effectiveness. (The main reason why the Prince-Sondheim musical, *Sweeney Todd*, didn't succeed—it clearly tried to be an American *Threepenny Opera*—is that it lacked a sharply defined political attitude toward the material and its stage presentation; it didn't go far enough into the realm of *performance*.)

3   Earlier in the century the special atmosphere and politics of European cabarets influenced the approach Brecht and Weill would take. There are several reasons why this is so, not the least of them the fact that the cabaret/club setting changes the relationship between audience and performer by forcing the performer to act in a more open, confrontational way, with less illusionistic dependence, not only because of the club's intimate spatial nature but because of its personality as a non-institutional space, private to its special audience, and beyond the bounds of official Culture to which it sets itself in opposition. Needless to say, it is more hospitable to forms of popular, immediate appeal, especially comedy. In this context, the growth of the music/performance scene in recent years is also related to the proliferation of clubs, the resurgence of interest in comic forms, and the acknowledgement of the audience's role in the making of theatre.

Contemporary musical styles, beginning with punk, then art rock and new wave, followed the same pattern of development vis-à-vis the audience. Today music is the new energy in avant-garde performance, a historical development which partly explains the popularity of Laurie Anderson—no small accomplishment when one realizes that up to now there had not been an American avant-garde performer or group whose theatre was rooted in music.

In the more popular, commercial music world Bette Midler and Peter Allen (incidentally, both started out in small clubs) at their best evolve performance styles that go beyond virtuosic display into sophisticated irony and self-parody that draws attention to the nature of superstar status. They put a distance between themselves and their material, talk about their own performance, at times even question audience response when it becomes too predictable, in all cases thriving on elaborately comic, campy banter that makes fun of media images of sex, fashion, power, and celebrity at the heart of the American culture industry. That their performance styles are non-traditional and the songs they sing rather straight-forward, often romantic, creates a further dialectic in the relationship of the on-stage performance personality to the songs themselves. (Barbra Streisand, who paved the way for Midler and Allen—as personalities—also showed the same ambiguity in her early years. Perhaps, what is really the question is how much these singers want their acts to be acceptable to the pop music world which all too easily co-opts and markets music's defiant gestures. They become less interesting to the degree that stage persona reflects the value system they oppose.)

But the expression of social attitudes and aggressive confrontation with audiences had already appeared years ago in the early jazz scene which grew out of the live setting, mostly clubs and private parties. Often jazz and blues singers would openly acknowledge the audience during their performance, in the traditional "call and response" pattern integral to the black experience of music. This speech/song technique was attractive to Weill who learned much from the rhythm and structure of jazz music whose fractured, syncopated beat was well suited to the disjunctive units of epic drama. That David Bowie has only recently appeared in a BBC production of Brecht's *Baal* shows that the development of "performance" as a musical style has come full circle in the breath of a new generation.

4 To extend the link further, the incorporation of talking in song is transformed in more narrative settings as cultural myth, sometimes as social criticism, in the operas of Anderson, Wilson, Glass, Monk and Ashley who've each taken the technique in different directions. It creates tension in the work between speech (documentary time) and song (poetic time) that is specifically dramatic, while also blurring distinctions between theatre, opera, poetry, and rock. At their most basic level Anderson's songs are detailed, satirical commentaries on American life, performed as clichés of everyday speech styles, Wilson and Monk evolve new poetics of sound in their language deconstruction, Ashley situates the feeling of space as myth in the mid-Western flatness of his voice, and Glass in his musical settings clarifies the social aspect of vocal music.

Voice and narrative have become important again in theatre, as a way to approach emotion, content, and social engagement in a live audience situation.

[1983-84]

The Young Barbra Streisand

THERE ARE PERHAPS TWO TIMES IN THE LIFE OF A SINGER, AT the beginning and at the end, when he or she overwhelms a piece of music, and absolutely nothing, no echo of a mask, intrudes between the singer and the song. It is true now of Sinatra, who makes love songs resonate in his bittersweet amber worldliness, just as it defined the young Streisand who was not yet worldly. In between, what gets one through is acting, the play of technique; and if there is too much reality of an emotional order, and yet a lack of truthfulness, a performance takes on a mannered tone, the expression of mere artifice. Singing is the voice's relationship to emotive life, and one regards its sincerity in the same terms that human gestures are scrutinized for their authenticity.

Perhaps inhabiting a song is, quite simply, an act of honesty. Or fragility. It is that perfect moment of art when personal vision and creative act join to give life to a new form that is more glorious than either of its parts. Whatever shape it takes, it is the most passionate, intense experience of song, the most deeply true. Like the adjectives on a person's face that describe its age, the sound of a voice also has a discernible history, a character. The voice of the young Streisand was the sound of blue and yellow watercolors. Her breathless, urgent rush through a phrase, flying over the tops of notes, flying through them, the way she would sing until she had no more of the song in her, almost heaving it out . . . She wouldn't hide it when she had to take a breath in the middle of a phrase, her insistent nasality made breathing a stylistic feature of her singing, sometimes transforming it into gasping. She'd spread the long, beautiful fingers of an outstretched palm over her stomach: was it to calm herself? To push the song out?

At other times the letting go of a note would be so luxurious and unhurried, it would seem to add seconds to the way musical time passes, as if this singer had all the time in the world. She sang with her mouth wide open, taking all the pleasures of song into her body, through her, and out again to the open air, her breath purifying the traveling sounds like a cool, fast mist. There was a purity in this young singer whose brilliance was so quick to give voice to its hunger. Not yet the deeper, harsher, clipped tones, the edge, the irony that appear in a voice when the singer and the song in her ages, and the longing has begun to have a history.

(On the night of June 17, 1967, I had tickets to see Judy Garland at a Long Island theatre. Instead, I went to see Barbra Streisand in Central Park's Sheep Meadow . . . Judy Garland would be around for a while, I'd see her another time . . . I remember Streisand's pink gown that unself-consciously abandoned itself to the wind while she sang. I remember the elegant tones that so completely swept through the park nature gave up the night to her. Sound and space came together to reorder the experience of time.)

It has been a long time since Streisand came to Central Park to sing the songs of a young woman and her simple fullness of desire. It was a long time ago, a glorious time . . . But even so, I have been a disloyal admirer. One can have a relationship with art—a book, a painting, a song—that grows from a profound kinship with the artist or work. (The great experience of art is aging with it and feeling it change through time inside you.) Yet, even as the art one creates for oneself sometimes dies, suddenly distraught at its insignificance, so the art that others create can die for one, too, though it may once have helped to intensify life. Streisand and I went our separate ways, we were no longer linked by a psychological moment, we aged, we found separate realities, we developed "artistic differences," we lived only in the past. That is part of the psychology of sound that outlines the attraction between music and its audience. If there is a certain pleasure in growing into and within the art of one's own time, there is also sadness, its opposite, in the disengagement (intellectual, emotional, ideological, sylistic) from an artist, that time can provoke unknowingly. Art is part of the education of the senses, we take from it what nourishes us and leave the rest to the metamorphosis of taste. To part from an artist is always a form of betrayal: Streisand no longer sings my songs (. . . and yet, this middle-aged Yentl attracts me again with the truthfullness of a voice that reflects new qualities of experience).

The body outlives certain feelings of the heart, especially the musical ones, those that acquire a mythic dimension in their linking of the stages of a life to pure states of being. Here one discovers emotional memory, always a bit askew for the lapse in time, but richer with every visit. If photographs frame the prose passages of a life, the record encompasses its poetry.

Privately, I return to earlier days in the sensual spaces of Streisand's voice that invite me in for a brief chance to recover lost images, and in the musical signatures that play with time, what was and what is, I roam around and read the songs that create my life.

[1983-84]

The Gal That Got Away
Judy Garland

IT WAS ON A TRAIN IN FLORENCE THAT I READ JUDY GARLAND had died. I would always buy *Time* to pass the hours of train travel though contemporary events seemed unextraordinary, even in so, it seems now, extraordinary a time as 1969. (Yet, was it not remarkable that I was on a train while a man was preparing to walk on the moon.) Such a present still could not measure up to the acts of history that one imagines were performed in the squares of a Renaissance city, and in its churches and palaces. Or was it simply a question of the kinds of space one is drawn to poetically, mine being old ruins rather than the site of an already ruined future. *Time* would temporarily connect me with events in America which, now that my back was turned to the Atlantic, existed as simply another foreign land I might dream of visiting someday, and that was a charming thought in the bracketed non-time one spends on a train, when one is neither here nor there. The train compartment would be my private theatre, a proscenium stage from which to view through its parted curtains the little dramas that take place in the aisles, or in the landscapes beyond the window frame. On this particular day I was preoccupied with the drama of a spent life.

None of the papers or magazines mentioned where she gave her last performance. In the rush to complete the scenario of her life, there was no time to stop and record where a singer, even Garland, sang her last song. It was Denmark (shall I say I was there to confirm that it happened?), not a capital among the geographical elite of musical places, only the modest country whose people gathered together to form her last public, in one of its suburbs, a train and a bus from the center of Copenhagen—in those days one could still take a trolley.

The clichés of celebrity life and neuroticism, the pills, the drugs, the unhappy love life. . . . (Oh, so familiar, the obituary for Tennessee Williams read the same.) Death notices of famous people are always written in advance, and like characters in a well-known play, their lives are fitted to the rigid conception of a role, for a public unwilling to accept new stagings of a life.

What stays in my mind is the topography of the performances: "I Can't Give You Anything but Love" downstage right, perched on the stage floor; "The Trolley Song" with the hand in the air; the walk along the edge of the stage, grazing outstretched hands attached to bodies that in a moment of spontaneous emotion, often erotic, lifted themselves out of their seats to run to her, hoping she might touch them. I remember the movie performances, how she used to sing with her whole body, the two arms like happy semaphores on either side, slightly bent outward from the body, breast high, leading the shoulders forward and back. (Today singers have mostly lost the use of their hands and arms as expressive features, attached as they are, puppet-like, to a microphone—but Garland, like Jolson and Merman, would sing with her arms. It was the kind of singing that commanded the body to live inside the song.) Even when she held a mike in one hand Garland distinctively moved the other, her left elbow creating a right angle where it joined the forearm, the back of a barely closed palm facing the audience . . . as if to draw the listeners to her in an invitational gesture. Audiences loved her need for them, and perceived her vulnerability in the geometry of that right angle.

Like all performers who inhabit a special emotional universe Garland had *presence*, the gift of life that insinuates the lives of performers into our own, a secret knowledge that can reorder the biological flow of life in another realm of existence. She loved to sing, she loved to laugh, she made smiling a part of singing. We experience being sung to in the rhythm of our bodies and there we return to the primal feelings that precede speech, to the language of imagery and abstract emotion, and perhaps to the childhood memory of a mother's song. Even the unborn can feel the sound of music, and we who are living find more life in it. Singing leads an audience back into personal reverie and then into a new feeling for life itself, a kind of journey into and through a landscape of wishes. The feeling of presence resides in the communal experience of art, it is a narcissism as it were, by which an audience sees in a performer a mirror image of itself in an ideal state, at the most heightened moment of physical sensitivity, beauty, and wholeness in space, as if real time were emptied of its urgency. There was a fullness in Garland that created air so thick with feeling it made your skin feel too small for your body, as if the body were taken by surprise at the luxurious stretching toward euphoria. Her singing filled a concert hall, the way only the human voice can, transforming it into a space that would envelop the audience who lived in her sound as people live in the sounds of nature. Her voice had the quivering loveliness and completeness of the sea. Sound that possesses you.

There is always something frightening in the way an audience loses control of itself at a concert, unknowingly to slip toward the emotions of mass hysteria. (The theatre is the natural place to study crowd psychology.) The remoteness of a singer on a stage, reinforced by the illusion of intimacy a singer promises, creates a dizzying eroticism in an audience, making this form of unrequited love all the more intense because there is no possible hope of fulfillment in relation to reality. It is desire fulfilled only in the world of aesthetics, imagination, a realm in which touch is absent. All that one can do at the end of a performance is to clap one's hands: this is all the touch that is allowed. Perhaps the difference between the way Europeans and Americans applaud live performance (Americans with their continuous, spontaneous rhythms, Europeans with their deliberate, measured claps) is the difference in their response to love as an aesthetic emotion. That possibility of going over the edge and losing oneself in the unattainable is all that makes art dangerously beautiful to the human spirit, it is its reckless charm. Who does not wish to live in art?

Can one measure the ecstasy song gives to the world, a pleasure all the more mysterious because it is invisible. One can watch a writer write, a painter paint, a musician play but how does one watch a singer sing, except to listen to a song that can never be seen, only taken on faith. Perhaps the wonder comes in watching the small universe of the open mouth shaping words in the air, the vibrating of the throat, the face dancing. Perhaps it is the sense of surrender in leaving the world of real things to live momentarily in the suspended consciousness of what is untouchable.

. . . On the train I thought of her death, what it means to lose certain artists of the world, to learn to forget a lyrical phrasing in song, just as the loss of a special rhythm of words comes with the death of a beloved writer. How would she have sung "Send in the Clowns"? . . . Does sound always live in the world? Will it turn time into space? Garland had left behind the world of my travels and entered another, a journey into time and memory, the twin poetries that conspire to create what we call history, or, looked at in another perspective, art. Was it so or did I dream, in a weary traveler's state of half-consciousness, that when the astronauts landed on the moon that July her voice had already whispered by, on the way to somewhere.

[1983-84]

Robert Wilson, The Avant-Garde, and The Audience
Einstein on the Beach

I

EINSTEIN ON THE BEACH WAS ONE OF THE MOST EAGERLY ANTIcipated theatrical events of this season. Premiered at Le Festival d'Avignon in France last summer, it was subsequently seen in Italy, Yugoslavia, Germany, Belgium, and Holland before being performed at the Metropolitan Opera House in New York, where it sold out two performances in November. Tremendous media-hype had preceded the presentation of the Robert Wilson-Philip Glass opera and, strangely, none of the critical establishment questioned the cultural anomaly of its engagement at the Met. More strangely, it was accorded the status of a masterpiece, though no critic has explained why.

Several people who have written about *Einstein* expressed the belief—good intentioned to be sure—that one could only *experience* the work, that analysis of it is either "inadequate" or "irrelevant," as if the simple act of coming to terms with the quality of the experience, or its nature, might somehow spoil its integrity as a Work of Art.

Such mindlessness on the part of critics, whose writings help shape the audience's attitude toward the arts, smacks of faddishness and ultimately creates an unhealthy situation in any attempt at prolonged discourse on the arts. This attitude makes the critics the cultural lackeys of artists in vogue, champions of a theatre they do not understand but feel they must praise because everybody is talking about it. Or worse, it turns critics into glorified press agents.

This strategy is, however, not surprising when one realizes that the avant-garde audience in New York is, in general, an *anti-intellectual* elite rather than an intellectual one. Soho's lofts and galleries are swarming with self-proclaimed artists (*L'art—c'est moi*) who are pampered by undiscriminating, ready-made audiences. The situation is damaging to any healthy arts environment, and encourages the false notion that anybody can be an artist (be he performer, dancer, filmmaker, video-artist, writer).

What we are witnessing in the large, cultish segment of avant-garde circles is the development of critics and audiences conditioned to relate to works of art on a purely personal, impressionistic level, as if the work had no relevance outside one's individual witnessing of it (a work of art means what it means to me), as if it had no relation to historical, social, economic, and aesthetic forces surrounding or preceding it. This is particularly true of the performing arts world, which has virtually reduced any discussion of performance to the simple level of description.

In choosing to ignore the cultural contradiction inherent in the mounting of *Einstein on the Beach* at the Met, most critics by-passed the real story, and demonstrated in the process the theatre world's lack of sophistication in dealing with the sociological aspects of theatre. Unlike the more sophisticated film, art, and music worlds, the theatre for the most part accepts art at face value.

The production of *Einstein* at the Met raises provocative questions about the current status of avant-garde (or experimental) theatre in America, not the least of which are: how has it changed? where is it headed? Indeed, with Wilson and Glass at the Met, Richard Foreman, Andrei Serban, and Jean-Claude van Itallie working at the Vivian Beaumont, and Tom Eyen and Charles Ludlam working on Broadway projects, not to mention the acceptance of experimental theatre by universities, foundations, and the media, to say that radical changes have taken place in the theatre since the sixties is a gross understatement.

Since its humble beginnings in oblivion, the avant-garde has developed to the point where it has found an audience and an ability to command attention and praise in establishment publications. Compared with its non-commercial, anti-establishment origins, the avant-garde has now formed new, and very commercial, alliances.

The real question should then be: can one speak any longer of an American avant-garde theatre? Present circumstances indicate that we are at the end of an era. The avant-garde, begun in opposition to the museum concept of the arts, has now been absorbed into the museum. Only The Living Theatre has consistently refused to become part of the Establishment and has been able to do so—even forced to—because of its politics. It exemplifies the original notion of the avant-garde—a union of art and politics that generally has not held in the twentieth century. Because of its politics The Living Theatre is "outside" today's avant-garde; the "inside" is bourgeois.

Robert Wilson exemplifies the inevitable destiny of the contemporary avant-garde artist in our society. His career illustrates the cycle of the artist: from oblivion to acceptance, from cultural nonentity to, literally, the "Talk of the Town" (*New Yorker*, December 6, 1976). An artist who once had to fight for his audience and his theatre now fills the Met twice over with a production that costs as much as a Broadway musical.

Wilson makes us question whether audiences have changed or whether certain segments of the avant-garde have become fashionable. In *The Dehumanization of Art*, Ortega y Gasset observed that "the characteristic of the new art, from a social viewpoint, consists of dividing the public into two classes of men: those who understand and those who do not." To update this observation one might include "those who do not understand but think they should." There is something terribly chic about the mounting of *Einstein* at the Met. As Renato Poggioli has pointed out, fashion is undeniably a factor in the sociology of taste. The avant-garde used to be characterized by *scandale*, now it is *au courant*. Robert Wilson has supped with the Shah of Iran.

The Wilson phenomenon forces one to confront the notion of avant-garde theatre and cultural chic; the topic hasn't arisen before now. But much has happened in the avant-garde since the last decade, not the least of which has been the ability of its most visible figure, Robert Wilson, to attract large segments of various art worlds, including individual patrons on both sides of the Atlantic. It is Wilson's patronage by the art world that facilitates his capacity to mobilize forces in a way that no other avant-gardist in the theatre has been able. For example: the "knee plays" from *Einstein* previewed at the Museum of Modern Art; a special program for the opera (it cost $10), more like a catalogue for an art exhibition, was financed personally by a member of the art world and sold at the Met; Wilson's drawings for *Einstein* were exhibited at the Paula Cooper Gallery. The "art" aspect of the event was reinforced by each of these situations.

It is Wilson's alignment with art business that makes his enterprise so unique when compared to the rest of the theatre world. The situation also illustrates an important point make by Eduardo Sanguineti in "The Sociology of the Avant-Garde": he notes the avant-garde's initial disdain for artistic commercialism, its gradual capitulation to it, and its eventual, paradoxical position at the forefront of the commercial organization of contemporary art. We are seeing a vast growth in the marketing capability of "art performance" (the video field is called "video art," likewise adding the "art" connotation to its name) here and abroad precisely because it is aligned with the art rather than with the theatre world.

It is difficult to speculate what will happen next to the avant-garde theatre, except that it will become more institutionalized. One thing is certain: it has consolidated its forces and become more sophisticated in its dealings with audiences, funding sources, and the media. Avant-garde artists have always wanted fame and recognition, which they have proved by their skillful manipulation of resources. Robert Wilson's evolution in the theatre over the last decade reflects the changes in attitudes on the part of the avant-garde.

II

"The history of the theatre is the history of the transfiguration of the human form," declared Oskar Schlemmer, no doubt alluding to his own Bauhaus creations as landmarks in theatrical history. Certainly, the artists who worked during the period between the wars did more to expand the vocabulary of the theatre than those at any other time in its history. Since the sixties, many experimentalists have enlarged upon the vocabulary of the Futurists, Dadaists, Bauhaus artists, Artaud, Meyerhold, Pirandello, and Brecht. We are at a point now where we can say again that the human figure has been transformed, that the notion of performance—indeed of theatre—has been reinterpreted.

One of the artists who has advanced theatre, because he has enlarged our vision of what theatre can be, is Robert Wilson. Wilson, however, is a difficult case because he is both a classicist and a modernist; his theatre is both beautiful and passive. It is also becoming more accessible as he gains popularity—and that is not a good sign.

Wilson had in the past named his productions after historical figures (Sigmund Freud, Joseph Stalin, Queen Victoria) but *Einstein on the Beach* is his most specifically historical piece simply because there is a direct link between what is being related in the opera (the destruction of the world through technological means) and the historical figure it is named after (Einstein, whose discoveries led to the bomb). Yet it remains a meditation on the modern age rather than an attempt to explore the life of Albert Einstein. Einstein is both inside (as a presence) and outside (playing his beloved violin from a position between stage and orchestra pit) the work, a witness to history on trial. Or is the opera offering a grotesque pun: the earth burned while Einstein fiddled?

Einstein on the Beach is an opera (though in no conventional sense) in four acts and nine scenes, constructed on the "assemblage" principle. It recalls many moments in art history, sorts out modern history at its pleasure, and develops a verbal text from a variety of sources that include pop music lyrics, the WABC round-the-clock disc jockey schedule, and the written speeches of cast members.

The composition of *Einstein* is defined by recurring structures of images, themes, gestures, and movements. Philip Glass's music is also a structure—mathematically precise—of repeating themes. The three central musical motives are linked to the three main images of the work: Train, Trial, Field. *Einstein* is so far removed from traditional opera that it becomes an anti-opera: whatever arias exist are verbal; the "libretto" consists of numbers or solfege syllables, the former standing for the rhythmic structure of the music, the latter for its pitch structure. Thus, in Act II there is what amounts to a parody of romantic opera in a couple's "La-Si-Do-Si-La-Fa,"etc. duet that ends with the woman shooting her partner.

Five "knee plays" or joints embody the opera's main spirit; these crucial episodes are expanded upon in the larger scenes of the work. For example, the design of knee play three pre-figures the geometric display of lights in the Act IV setting of a Spaceship interior. The fifth knee play offers a major theme of the opera—albeit the simple politics of its "message" of peace and love—when two figures (after the bomb) appear as lovers on a bench in the moonlight. They represent the new society.

The central theme—the loss of innocence in the modern age—is not unique to *Einstein*; it is merely a new visualization of the same theme that appeared in *A Letter for Queen Victoria* and *The $ Value of Man*. But here the theme is more concretely realized in the specificity of the subject matter (the movement of images from locomotive to spaceship) and remains dominant throughout the opera. The Field scenes at the center of the opera, Acts II and III, clearly simulate the playfulness of an idyllic, pre-technological existence before the holocaust (*Queen Victoria* worked along the same lines, though less explicitly; *$ Value* featured a "garden of Eden" scene). Conversely, the knee plays depict images of mechanized, modern existence. In these segments, as in the contemporary scenes throughout the opera, performers are dressed as Einstein (in neutral colored pants, shirts, and suspenders) while in the Field sequences they wear more colorful and varied clothing. The difference between the two moments in history is thus accented in the costuming.

One can contrast the rigid, mechanical movements of Lucinda Childs and Sheryl Sutton pressing dials and controls in the knee plays with the looseness of the performers' movements in the two Field sequences. In the latter, people enjoy and are conscious of the rhythms of their bodies; their faces are free of fixed expression and they seem full of abandon. Yet the Spaceship lurks in the distance and will appear in the scenes from contemporary life.

The symbolic transformation of movement from one scene to another signals the importance of *gestus* in Wilson's conception of stage language. Witness Lucinda Childs's robot-like, jagged arm movements and frenzied marching steps in Act I—her diagonal dance—while behind her a second performer moves mechanically in a straight line, and still others construct a triangle of string. The performer is not used for his imitative or psychological qualities, but for his materiality, his potential as sculptural form. The performer, then, does not imitate; he serves as a symbol. Gesture and movement are always symbolic, reflecting the neo-Platonism of this theatre that replaces discursive language with a grammar of symbols. One confronts spatial and gestural motives instead of dialogue. Looking at the performers in their surroundings, one realizes how much of an architect Wilson is.

In light moments one can think of Wilson as the Inigo Jones of the avant-garde. The two men share a grandiose sense of spectacle, a delight with the movement of bodies in space, and an interest in masks or "doubles." Moreover, the notion of theatre as an event for socializing is also significant; a nearly five hour intermissionless opera, *Einstein* provided the spectator with his own choice of when to take a break and wander the lobbies of the Met. Clusters of "socializing" spectators were to be seen throughout the performance. With *Einstein* Wilson has also refunctioned the concept of the masque, the form to which Jones was devoted, to make it a modern allegory. Perhaps one can even consider the Patty Hearst segment of *Einstein* (in the Trial scene) as an anti-masque—a grotesque inversion of the "trial" of Einstein.

Wilson's classicism and modernism are in continual conflict, which only serves to emphasize his anarchy of form. There are so many "quotations" of art in *Einstein* that one might seriously ask if Wilson is a mannerist. One sees the concern for line, the architectural clarity of Gordon Craig who, like Wilson, stressed the importance of *seeing* in the theatre as opposed to listening; certainly Wilson's depersonalization of the performer reflects Craig's concept of the *über-marionette*. Act I (Trial) offers a visual pun in its placement of a bed downstage that concretizes the image of a slide shown behind the judge's table of the "bed of justice" (*lit de justice*), an actual trial at Versailles in 1776 (engraving after Girardet).

And yet, as quickly as one recognizes these elements, one is confronted with quotes from the Bauhaus school: the modernist furniture used in the knee plays and the entire set-up of the courtroom (discs, rectangles, triangles) in the Trial scene. Wilson's design for the judge's table looks like Moholy-Nagy; his use of light-in-motion even more so. In Act IV, a bed of light, so called because one side of the rectangular structure is lighted, slowly disappears into the flys, but not before reminding us of a work of minimal art. And what to do with the near replication of The Living Theatre's *Frankenstein* set for the Spaceship design in the last act of the production?

Inorganic, ostentatious, self-conscious, stylistically confusing, an art of defor-mation—*Einstein on the Beach* is all of these. Perhaps the best justification for Wilson's theatre is to be found in Arnold Hauser's insight into mannerism as an outgrowth of alienation. He defines mannerism as "the product of tension between classicism and anti-classicism . . . rationalism and irrationalism, sen-sualism and spiritualism, traditionalism and innovation, conventionalism and revolt against conformism."

Wilson's alienation from the realities of contemporary life is precisely the im-petus for his theatre that finds a home in the mythopoeic tradition of the American avant-garde. Wilson's recent pieces have used contemporary myths to illustrate his dissatisfaction with the alienation of modern life. His vision is apocalyptic; he seeks a return to order and peace after the holocaust. Is this not a reflection of Romantic longing for a return to a world that we will never see again? Wilson's handling of contemporary problems is too naive to take seriously.

Wilson's escapism is the problematical element in his theatre. The danger is that audiences, overwhelmed by the monumental settings and the beauty of the images, will be passively drawn into the spiritualistic world of his theatre, which in peculiar ways mirrors the growing mass consciousness of the seventies. It is one that reflects surrender. Critics and audiences have admitted that they see *Einstein on the Beach* as a work one must give oneself up to. Indeed one does not have to be conscious of the proceedings on stage. The sensuality of the imagery, the repeating, glorious chords and high volume of Glass's music (it has been called "trance" music), and the spinning, dervish choreography of Andy DeGroat all contribute to make *Einstein on the Beach* an experience of transcendental meditation in the theatre.

It is this sense of loss of time and place, the religiosity of the experience, the absorption in images that by their nature are ambiguous, simple resolutions of harsh political realities, and the acceptance of a theatre that hypnotizes its devout followers that is disturbing. It is indeed questionable whether Wilson will lead us to higher consciousness. Theatre must be more than something to gape at or lose oneself in.

[1977]

Our Town Our Country
The Wooster Group on Route 1 and 9

IF YOU FOLLOW ROUTE 1 ALL THE WAY NORTH FROM NEW Jersey you'll end up in Vermont, the landscape of Thornton Wilder's *Our Town* which is the center(piece) of The Wooster Group's *Route 1 and 9 (The Last Act)*. The intersection of these two sensibilities—Wilder's genteel view of small town America at the turn of the century and the Group's more abrasive contemporary politics—generates a new text whose subject is "our country."

Wilder is, I think, the unacknowledged early link to avant-garde theatre. When most of his contemporaries were busy devising literal *settings* for their plays, he was already working out the idea of *performance space*: in that differentiation lies the history of experimentation in American theatre. Early on Wilder understood how space, as a highly artificialized property, could be constructed during the performance itself, a project he put into practice and which The Wooster Group has carried on. The notion of building a space has always been important in the Group's aesthetic, acting as conceptual backbone of its anarchic union of forms and raw-edge emotions: their productions force audiences to watch how they are being put together because the *process of making theatre* won't let itself be taken for granted.

In *Route 1 and 9* the performance is very rigorously delineated in four segments which, briefly, are these: "The Lesson" (on video tape), "The Party" and a romantic scene from *Our Town*, "The Last Act" which is the final scene of *Our Town*, and an overlapping explicitly sexual video tape that plays off the porno genre and "Route 1 and 9" film. The cross cutting of film and live action from two rhythmically different performance "texts" creates the dialectical "frame" of reference this difficult, disturbing work evolves, and to which Elizabeth LeCompte gives so startling a directorial shape.

Ron Vawter opens the production with a satiric reconstruction of a 1965 Encyclopedia Britannica film lesson which demonstrates how to interpret *Our Town*—this is the way most of us were taught play analysis in school. His purposefully fatuous and wooden impersonal delivery challenges the whole system of Cartesian logic, in fact the humanist tradition of interpretation itself, by which knowledge is transmitted in the culture. The speech doesn't by itself mock the play, but the comically gestural, old-fashioned acting style in which it is delivered only serves to show the aesthetic distance we've traveled through modernist art and theory: the classical approach to interpreting drama is too codified and stale for an open system work such as *Route 1 and 9*. Set against this "lesson" is the alternative model of the "learning play" (in the specific Brechtian sense of the term) that the Group proposes.

Video is used again for a romantic scene (in close-up) between a young couple in Wilder's play. What is remarkable about this scene, played in an intense, soap opera acting style, is its inherent commentary on language, chiefly the distinctions between stage language and film language, but beyond that theatrical dialogue and the more natural speech that has replaced it in avant-garde theatre, and finally, pointing up the differences between acting and performing. Quite simply, the highly charged expressive language that Wilder's characters speak overwhelms video technology. I found myself watching a monitor furthest from where I was sitting because the dialogue was too powerful, perhaps "full" is more correct a word, for a film medium. (Theatre productions fail on television precisely because of this disproportionate sense of scale in the speech.) What's more, I realize how much I regret the absence of inflected, unself-conscious stage speech.

Some of the actors in this video love scene re-emerge in the sex film segment (e.g., Willem Dafoe is both the young George of *Our Town* and the randy male), in the sequence in which whites in blackface variously set up the space for the next scene (Wilder's stage hands also prepare the cemetery scene), drink, dance, party and call up take-out food places (here real time intrudes on artificial time), and in the car ride of the closing film. A few (including the actor who gives the opening "lesson") also recreate a Pigmeat Markham comedy routine ("The Party") originally performed by the famous black comedian in 1965.

In the context of *Route 1 and 9* this latter scene functions as a double commentary on the concept of the mask that by its form criticizes the idea of playing roles, both in society and in theatre. It is also a radical use of the theatrical *masque* ("a form of entertainment originally featuring the arrival of guests in disguise bearing gifts"—the *Encyclopedia of World Theatre* precisely defines the blackface segment), that illuminates the real content of the piece.

Route 1 and 9 is filled with such contrasting and distorting mirrors, all of them reflecting perspectives on the manner of American life and death: the "journey" theme of *Our Town* juxtaposed with the "Route 1 and 9" film segment that shows characters in a hapless car ride through the polluted industrial New Jersey landscape (I think the addition of quotations from Wilder's *Happy Journey to Trenton and Camden*, poised in relation to that film, would have contributed an even more ironic frame to the piece—but that is a personal view); the memory of Wilder's childlike lovers erased by the film's faceless, copulating figures whose only language is a genital one; stage hands who provide a historical continuum to the scenes; the conventional drama lesson lost in the radical dramaturgical model this piece proposes. Uniting all these aspects is *Our Town's* last scene, set in a cemetery, whose inhabitants act as a chorus commenting on the live action as it moves through time.

Route 1 and 9 embodies an uncompromising critique of prescribed social and art forms that outlines, from Wilder to the present, the loss of innocence, of spontaneous expression, communication and language, of values. That energetic critique is the unspoken dialogue the two texts compose: the Wilder text, by its very "quotation," is the system against which the whole production can be measured. One also finds constructed in it an American experimental theatre history: of acting syles, organization of space, use of props, multiple role playing, theatrical language. And in Jim Clayburgh who, with LeCompte designed the production, one sees Wilder's stage manager for the new theatre he envisioned, cranking up the television sets for a change of scene.

Route 1 and 9 is in that line of the best world tradition of the avant-garde that is both politically and aesthetically radical. In this country only The Living Theatre, Squat, guerilla theatre groups and black theatres of the sixties have approached audiences with the high energy assault tactics that these theatres have made characteristic of their work. Their antecedents are found in the classical avant-garde line of dadaists, futurists, and surrealists who valued the gesture—the theatrical action—above all else: theatre that undercuts the assumed values of its own form as well as subverting institutionalized thinking. This is theatre as an act of faith in the power of art to change people.

There has been much controversy as to whether *Route 1 and 9* is racist, an accusation leveled at it by audiences, critics and the consensus of the New York State Council on the Arts which, it seems certain, has withheld funding for that particular work of the Group's because of its blackface scene. This potentially dangerous judgment, now under appeal, is an insult to the Group, but more than that a grave matter for all the issues it raises with regard to the censorship of experimental art, interpretation and intentionality, artistic criteria, and the relationship of the avant-garde to public funding demands.

Route 1 and 9 has to be analyzed within the Group's history and development of techniques and themes that define its style: distortion, exploration of character types, juxtaposition of several art forms, masking, identity crises, demystifying social and family traditions of white America, satiric and ironic modes of performance, play-within-play structures, deconstruction of space—there is nothing that leads logically to the charge of racism. Unless one considers an *anti-white* stance racist.

This work ruthlessly depicts the disintegration of white American society, and the perversion of its manners and values. It attacks the mode of thinking on which Western civilization is founded—even mocking accepted ways of thinking, feeling, talking, creating art, and finally, living. It's been a long time since any avant-garde theatre in New York presented a politically controversial work of such emotional ferocity. We had forgotten that this kind of work should generate polemical outbursts in audiences.

This is why the question of racism is such a stupidly myopic entree into an analysis of the piece. Does putting actors in blackface mean that the work is racist? Is racism only about color? Does putting a female character in an apron mean a play is sexist? When does a Jewish mother become an anti-Semitic figure? And, my last point, if whites are exaggerated comic figures or stereotypes in plays by blacks, is that a form of racism—or is it affirmative action? If the idea of *representation* is undermined it destroys the foundations on which theatre is based.

To my mind, the only positive actual scene in the whole piece is the metaphoric segment with the blacks, their masque that masks the real allegory of *Route 1 and 9* and links it to the house—the partially-built aluminum stud structure whose very presence criticizes the box set and the ideology of traditional domestic realism that it alludes to in this scene and in all the Group's previous work. That *house* that is not a home is the elusive sense of place LeCompte has theatricalized from an abstract ideal. *Route 1 and 9* is a poetic statement about leaving home (that of the parents—and for LeCompte it was literally New Jersey) and trying to establish an independent base. It has to do with stability, roots/routes, a place in society (for the endless oppressed the "black face" represents) but in particular for the artist as outcast. *Route 1 and 9* is a triumph of survival without capitulation to social and artistic expectations.

The only language of this work is Wilder's: his beautiful, evocative language, now so lost to us it actually sounds more like literature than everyday speech, so far away because it reminds us of the absence of sustained verbal discourse in contemporary life. *Route 1 and 9* sets off a desperate cry for communication. Is anybody listening?

"Perhaps all religions die out with the exhaustion of language," Wilder once wrote, as if he could see from a more peaceful American era the coming despair that would separate the body from language because it became futile to talk.

[1982]

Encounters

The Politics of Performance

THE IMPACT OF RICHARD SCHECHNER'S PROVOCATIVE ARTICLE ("The Decline and Fall of the [American] Avant-Garde"*), arriving at a time when audiences are becoming noticeably reflective about theatrical experience, seems all the more significant because it articulates the position of an avant-garde theatre that is becoming increasingly conscious of itself and its image. I don't agree with Schechner's assessment of the avant-garde from the perspective of "decline" and "fall" because there is more to this crisis than the life cycle he describes.

The "path of interculturalism" that he proposes for its rebirth misses the point, I think, because it seeks generalized solutions outside American culture, in the archetype, when what the avant-garde theatre community (its artists and audiences) needs to do now is to analyze its particular position vis-à-vis its own culture and institutions. How is it perceived? How does it perceive itself? That is the starting point for my response.

Consider the relationship of avant-garde theatre and the press. If one believes, as I do, that it is in a period of self absorption, it does not come as a surprise that all of the artists who responded to Schechner addressed the subject of critics and the press (Lee Breuer had intended to write a long article on theatre criticism but he could not complete it in time for publication). Ruth

---

*My essay was a response to Richard Schechner's "The Decline and Fall of the (American) Avant-Garde" which he had published in *Performing Arts Journal*, Numbers 14 and 15, 1981. There were also responses by Ruth Maleczech, Elizabeth LeCompte, Spalding Gray, and Matthew Maguire in the subsequent issue of *PAJ*.

Maleczech writes of "hating the critics who keep you poor," Elizabeth LeCompte laments the lack of "critical support," Spalding Gray complains that it took "six phone calls to get a *Voice* critic to come see *A Personal History of the American Theatre*," and Matthew Maguire, the youngest of the three and therefore the most representative of the way the coming generation regards the situation, sees Schechner's views as potentially "discouraging of fundraising."

If they had discussed theatre criticism in a less self-centered context it might have been beneficial to all of us as a genuine public exploration of how "avant-garde theatre" is perceived in the media and in the public eye. Instead, taken together, the replies give the impression that their authors view critics and criticism/reviewing (they are not differentiated) as a scapegoat responsible for avant-garde theatre's lack of serious attention in the culture, its financial insecurity, and all that that implies in terms of "career."

These assumptions about the role and function of critics frame the discussion unhealthily in the realm of economics, as if any commentary that does not support a work or movement jeopardizes its value in the marketplace. It is no longer possible to conceive of reviews of performances as merely news because of the function they have, and the way they are perceived in the "performance industry" that avant-garde theatre has become. The widespread competitiveness of performers and theatre groups for media coverage, and the relationship of coverage to the event and to money, should be a signal for everyone to stop and think about what "avant-garde" theatre is, and where it is heading.

If those who make theatre view writing about theatre—of course, I am only speaking of intelligent writing, not the uninformed review—exclusively in terms of public relations (that is, in a way that will enhance their image and thus their monetary value) then they have lost sight of the real value of serious, public dialogue on the art. The avant-garde theatre, those who write about it and its audience, is starved for any authentic, intelligent exchange of ideas. Not only the theatre piece or text, but any serious theatre writing about it that appears, confronts a great big void because virtually nothing has any impact on anyone. The value of Schechner's article is that it broke through this terrible, deadening silence.

Theatre artists, I think, are ignoring the real and deeper causes of their alienation, first blaming the press, then later turning to it as if it were a *deus ex machination* that could save their image and their career. They overvalue its relation to their survival when the problems lie elsewhere. It seems that now is the time for everyone to move away from naive opinion to a genuine understanding of the politics of performance—specifically, to analyze theatre's modernist position in the culture, and the forces that challenge it.

Of course, the main reason why this theatre is obsessed with the press is obvious: the economics of producing theatre (much of it highly technological and expensive), has made contemporary theatre court public praise which builds audiences and grant possibilities (foundations are heavily influenced by the press) which help to finance new work. This process of de-evolution describes the credit system that theatre binds itself to, creating a permanent welfare class of financially unstable artists (Schechner ably documents the financial troubles of The Performance Group in his article) to whom grant subsidy gives a false sense of security, and an even falser hope for a "career" in the American theatre. Even Joseph Papp cannot save avant-garde theatre.

Its members tour Europe, teach, give workshops, lecture—to supplement grant subsidy and unemployment benefits—all of which take them away from the practice of their "profession" which is to create new work. All around them they see experimenters in other art forms making money from their work, gaining acceptance, and more and more finding a place in the culture, and in the critical discourse of their art. (Philip Glass and Laurie Anderson are two current examples of experimental artists who are becoming increasingly accepted in the public eye. It happens to painters and to writers, too, but not to people in the theatre.) Long past the time they should be established professionals they are still in the bread line for grants.

For the first time in this country there is an avant-garde theatre whose most influential artists are middle-aged, still "outsiders," yet operating as if they were on the inside. The reason this situation occurred, and will continue to, is that in American society theatre has no stable base in the intellectual community, no significance except as a pastime and, in fact, is alienated from the literary community, the one sector that can legitimize it, because of its ambiguous relationship to the dramatic text as literature.

Intellectuals have ignored the American theatre after Edward Albee: playwriting deteriorated with a few exceptions, and the most original theatrical minds turned to creating collective texts and performance theory which have no value in the literary community. An avant-garde cannot really succeed, if only emotionally, when it does not have the strong support of a community who shares its ideals and who can join it in countering the status quo. The sense of rage that the theatre world feels is mainly a lack of a sense of place in the culture.

Yet, on the surface it seems as if avant-garde theatre has a place in shaping thought in culture. How is it treated in the press? In America there are three theatre journals which give partisan support to the avant-garde on a regular basis (*Performing Arts Journal*, *The Drama Review*, *Theater*), even the more academic *Theatre Journal* prints an occasional piece on it; the New York *Times*, *Village Voice*, *Villager*, *Soho Weekly News*, *Other Stages*, *Saturday Review* and *New Republic* all review or feature avant-garde work, none of it written by anyone who is especially out "to get" the avant-garde. Avant-garde theatre in New York—I can't speak for elsewhere—is suffering from media overkill. Too much exposure is making it an expendable commodity while not really enhancing its cultural role.

This familiarity has bred a certain contempt among avant-gardists who justifiably are exasperated by reviewers who write on them with no sense of their past work, its evolving situation, and scant knowledge of its aesthetic concepts. At the same time, none of the major literary periodicals (*New York Review of Books, Partisan Review, Salmagundi,* and so on) publish articles on contemporary American theatre. This same intellectual community that can find members who support other difficult new ideas and aesthetics never came into the theatre when its most important thinkers turned to creating performance theory instead of dramatic literature. It is more than a mind/body split. It has to do with the finding and losing of a language.

The emergence of a new theatrical language in the last twenty years of American theatre has led to a sharp break in theatrical criticism which has always been based on the *interpretation of texts,* more precisely, on Aristotelian poetics. This crisis—and it truly is one for the theatre and its audience—that theatrical criticism faces developed because recent theatre has created a new language that has challenged all the conventional ideas about seeing, writing, performing, designing, and perceiving theatre. It is forced to exist outside a critical discourse. There is no evolving radical theory of performance or drama within the American intellectual tradition. Conversely, film, rock music, and dance, all of them younger than theatre, already have an established critical language. When critics write about these forms they can situate themselves in a historically expanding discourse that is fed by both critics and art.

Avant-garde theatre does not have this ongoing dialogue with itself. And like it or not, only what is written about will remain a part of theatrical tradition, and those who write about it shape the opinions of future generations. The absence of critical and theoretical books (with few exceptions) on avant-garde theatre, the absence of a history of performance are indicative of this historical void it is falling into.

The highly individualistic temperament of American theatre—now regarded worldwide for the innovations of its theatrical vocabulary and break from traditional theatre—is what attracts so many Europeans who come here, to work in theatre, or simply to watch, but mainly to escape the oppressive language of their own theatres which are bound to codified and institutionalized discourse. In Germany, all playwriting must reckon with the Brechtian tradition, and one compares this year's production of *Antigone* with last year's, and the years before that. Oppositely, avant-garde theatre here has gotten so self-referential that it can manipulate the terms of critical discourse. Real—not artificial—discourse presupposes a link with a common language, not a private language that continually rarefies its manner of speaking. The problem for criticism in avant-garde theatre is that we have no performance *language* that is specifically theatrical, that is not anthropological, not literary, not filmic, not psychoanalytic, not philosophical. And I'm not sure there can ever be one because the human body, the actor, is always *representational:* he will always remind the critic of the world beyond the stage.

The crisis of avant-garde theatre is partly explained by the crisis of modernism. We are in a transition period today that registers the change in the way the avant-garde perceives itself, and the way it is perceived by the public. We are confronted by a media network that co-opts artistic rebellion and experiments in search of the news scoop, a popular culture whose activities increasingly parallel certain ideals of the avant-garde, and a government and corporate structure that gives financial support to an avant-garde industry—entirely non-profit—by virtue of its tax laws.

For the last fifteen years at least literary critics and social scientists have written on the impossibility of being "avant-garde" in the liberal society of advanced capitalism. Bourgeois culture imitates modernist aesthetics and attitudes so openly in its obsession for self-expression and the new that the concept of "avant-garde" has been drained of its original meaning. It's gotten to the point now that it is difficult to discover who's imitating who. Bourgeois culture *is* the avant-garde. One can no longer underestimate its talent for absorbing innovation. Perhaps the push by certain critics and artists to define a "post-modern" age is at its root a need to rid the twentieth century of modernism while still maintaining the goals of a vanguard. If the avant-garde can't be modernist, it can be post-modern. Democracy will yet make artists of all its people.

Since there is virtually no public theoretical dialogue on theatre, especially with regard to the avant-garde, there is no continuing critique of its position in the culture. Yet, more than any other art form, theatre is most implicated in everyday life because of this culture's infatuation with *performance* as a means of personal awareness and expression, as life style. Now that the *theatrical* is recognized as a way of being in the world, how will *theatre* think of itself?

My final point is, Can one speak any longer of an "avant-garde theatre" when this theatre is institutionalized and domesticated, of its own will and lack of revolt, by its own culture? How absurd that our "avant-garde" theorist/ spokesman is a tenured professor in this country's wealthiest university—NYU, the only place to go if you want to grow up and be an avant-gardist—and whose research in India on "interculturalism" is financed by Rockefeller money! I mention these facts not to make a fool of Schechner—I admire his sense of engagement and willingness to speak out on issues when no one else will—simply to demonstrate how perverse is the relationship of avant-garde theatre to its society.

Avant-garde theatre has got to reinvent itself at this juncture of art/history: it can be the loud, thoughtful voice of a radical critique (political and aesthetic) of culture, it can go underground, or it can cry itself to sleep.

Those who believe in the avant-garde imagination should become more actively engaged in a continuing critique of avant-garde theatre and its place in society. What I am suggesting is a *process*, not a program of thought. Schechner is absolutely correct that "polemics" are a necessary aspect of a healthy theatre.

I'd like to see artists discuss each other's work and their own work, the theories of critics, and their audiences—not to turn them into critics but rather to force an awareness of what it means to be doing theatre now. I'd like to see writers develop a new criticism, rethink the historical assumptions about theatre and drama, and create new histories of theatre.

All of us should question the patterns of funding, audience reception, the attitudes of producing organizations, and the directions in performance and writing, in a continuing public dialogue of how we feel about theatre in this time and in this place.

Notes on A Poetics of Performance

performance as a way of life

Schechner's belief in the theatrical as "a primary human activity" is bound up with an idea of performance as social function—performance as ritual, healing, shamanism—that is, theatricalized activity whose purpose is *to communicate*. The concept of "performance" in its more up to date manifestations has gone beyond Schechner's confining, even classical, definition to mean much less a communicative activity than a conceptualizing of oneself as a therapeutic survival tactic. Today we can learn more about the need for theatricalized activity from Pirandello and Genet than from sociologists and anthropologists. Schechner's own theory of performance is not rooted enough in a *theatrical language*—it derives too much from structural anthropology.

Americans are obsessed with self-expression because the options for creative self-expression in an affluent society are limitless. The idea that one can make oneself up is liberating, even possible. It is also very "American" in that it allows one to believe in the possibility of a life lived outside of a history (be it personal, social, political).

All of today's "how to" and "self help" books are about creating images of yourself, not for the purpose of communicating, but to get by; not for the purpose of developing any continuing reality but to relate to shifting "realities." Schechner's notion of performance activity presupposes a belief in an order that gives all human activity a frame in society, as if theatrical activity were entirely structured by social order (by the community). On the contrary, "performance" as a way of being in the world is an *ad hoc* path to self awareness and fulfillment, and it is becoming more dominant because no one has a safe place in society anymore, there is no social order (community). The only chance to retain a degree of freedom of expression is to upstage everyone else.

The concept of "performance" increasingly dominates American culture as a way of viewing everyday activity. It is, for example, encouraged as a therapeutic technique, and used to describe sexual activity, the operation of a car, a politician's form, business management style. Media commentary is increasingly attuned to describing behavior in theatrical terms, as if all human action was incapable of being anything other than artificial. Now that the culture is infatuated with spectacle, communication is more and more conceived of as *gesture*. Language is losing its ability to express collective belief; performance is a private language which when acted out publicly evolves as imagery.

The incursion of the media into every realm of experience has sabotaged the notion of "privacy": the *media as public eye* has forced the private I onto a world stage. This growing dramatization of every moment has caused the public in general to act as if an audience—potentially the entire world—were watching. Life is then viewed entirely in theatrical terms: that is, the existence of a performer and an audience is presupposed.

The cruelest imagery is the appropriation of a theatrical vocabulary which describes "nuclear theatre," now discussed in the press as if it were an upcoming major production. It is treated as a kind of morality play in which the whole world acts out the final cosmic drama—all the stage is the world. The creation of the term "nuclear theatre" (much more specific than the Army's generalized definition of "European theatre" and "theatre of war") is an imperialist use of language that decides who will be the spectators and the actors in this grotesque drama. On November 5, 1981, the front page of the New York *Times* reported the possibility of an upcoming dress rehearsal, which officialese euphemistically refers to as a "demonstration" of nuclear weapons.

technique and tradition

The refusal of avant-garde artists to work on texts not created by their own group is on one level an obsession with individual ownership, with property. By not acknowledging the world dramatic heritage they deny the possibility that plays can be "new" in successive historical periods. To work creatively on a classical text is not merely to "interpret" it—that is a restrictive view of making theatre—but to create a new text. Ideas in a work don't belong to artists anyway, they belong to the world.

In his early writings, Schechner proselytized for the removal of the playwright from the theatre. Now he laments, "however much we may have attacked the line from Stanislavski through Boleslavski to Clurman and Strasberg . . . such a line of descent exists. My generation failed to develop the means of training artists." Schechner, I think, overlooked the degree to which theatrical tradition is carried in the literature of theatre which is at its core society's history, its language.

There is a Brechtian *tradition* because Brecht wrote plays that can be staged and rethought in new historical periods. Grotowski, on the other hand, has no more influence in the *making* of theatre, except as a kind of guru, because his technique became outmoded when rigorous body training ceased to interest theatre groups. Technique doesn't have the regenerative power that dramatic language does.

The limitations of a theatre built on performance theory is that it only evolves a *technique,* not a tradition. While a few others than the originators have done avant-garde texts, they are not easily absorbed into the dramatic repertoire which is what ultimately generates a tradition in theatre.

Schechner's vision of "interculturalism" is founded on the premise that one can transport tradition through technique, "body-to-body," as he sees it. But, tradition stays within its own country, only the technique travels.

We have reached a point in the development of the theatre where technique is easily passed on or acquired through a vast world-wide network. (The influence of Grotowski in the sixties attests to that.) Often I think there is only technique, that theatre is not created out of need, only know-how, that technique triumphs over imagination. Much of the work today has a hollowness inside because there is no authentic emotional life, only artifice.

recent history

Contemporary experiments in theatre outline a history of displacements: the playwright superseded by the director/group, discursive language by the image, dialogue by the monologue, the ensemble by the solo performer. This constant throwing away of what is theatrical is, in its own way, an anti-theatrical impulse. What to do with an art that is always becoming something other than itself, always deconstructing its own language?

Avant-garde art movements in the twentieth century have a tradition of doing "performance" without dealing with theatre. The denial of illusion, of representation, finally of a shared language, has been the program of performance as exemplified by art world values.

Performance art is an anti-theatrical form that displaces illusion with real time, character with personality, skill with spontaneity, artifice with the banal. It values idea over execution; the artist and his/her idea is more important than the work itself which has no autonomy outside of its creator and the moment of its creation. It is a kind of throwaway art that in an odd way links up with the cabaret tradition of the classical avant-garde.

Schechner's dismay at the lack of new faces in theatre only serves to show he is looking in the wrong places, besides using an outdated definition of performance. Most of the younger generation doing performance is more tuned in to the art and music worlds than the theatre world. That this movement is essentially anti-theatrical is another matter.

The devaluation of expressive language in avant-garde theatre has reached such a point that the shock of The Wooster Group's *Route 1 & 9* is not its blackface routine that some audiences and press questioned as racist, or its blatantly cheap porno movie, but the experience of hearing language with real emotional content—in the videotaped cemetery scene from *Our Town* that is spliced into the piece—in the theatre. How perverse that hearing people talk to each other in a shared language should now be so jolting a theatrical event.

When I listen to the instrumental music of Philip Glass I feel I am *in sound.* Usually, one experiences a concert as a division between the auditorium and the stage, as if one were *watching* it. Listening to Glass one is in it and of it, consumed by the shimmering beauty and spirit of the moment. One is forced to *experience* it because of its commitment to total saturation.

The popularity of the music coincides with an American cultural moment when a large strain of the population is seeking absorption in the world of the spirit, and the transcendence of the material world that promises. Glass's music—it brings real emotion into music theatre—is "another look at harmony" that challenges the discordant, anguished modernist music that has dominated experimentation in this century. It searches out the world inside the body, the wholeness and emotion of experience, in repetitive structures that are soothing, unified, meditative, demanding one to surrender to it. If musical form has a politics, and I believe it does, Glass exemplifies the move away from the aggressiveness of Western music (the modernist line and rock) and toward the Eastern recognition of sound as life flow. More than that, challenging the conventional notion of time as measurable, it alludes to infinite sound.

When I first saw the Squat Theatre in a secret performance in Budapest in 1975, it was the first time I was part of an audience for whom the mere fact of attendance was a radical act. Their life as artists conditioned them to value the relationship of theatre and society for the moral imperative it could give their work. Squat is a rarity in theatre in that it operates according to the original definition of "avant-garde" art: radicalism in politics and in art. Squat creates as if there is a tomorrow.

The Squat Theatre is "old-fashioned" in the contemporary context: the group still believes in the subversive possibilities of theatre. If the main current of theatrical experimentation is involved in art about art, Squat, following in the European tradition, makes art that is about the audience—that is, social relations. It *involves* the audience in a radical critique of cultural assumptions by implicating it in its criticism. Likewise, by understanding—as outsiders —American culture and its consumption of its imagery, their work is able to articulate an attitude, even an analysis, of the theatrical imagery they create, rather than simply producing more images.

The most exaggerated forms of theatricality, even operatic form, are found today in American and German work (respectively, in theatre and film), not surprisingly since the move toward performance is a distinct development in affluent cultures whose "reality" is most fabricated by the media and mythmaking. In the films of Hans-Jürgen Syberberg, Jean-Marie Straub and Rainer Werner Fassbinder, to give some examples, theatricality is used to situate an analysis of oppression in the critique of society as artificial form. Theatricality is used as a way to understand the illusions of freedom, how power is given representational form in the roles people assume. Essentially, theatricality is viewed as a model of social behavior that criticizes society. It is a kind of corrective comedy form.

The most radically innovative theatre I have ever seen is not theatre, but Syberberg's film *Our Hitler* whose structure presupposes the *presence* of a thinking audience. *Our Hitler* is a film that was staged (film does not often imitate theatre!) in a totally artificial (unfilmic) performance style that is narrative (Brechtian). The filmic frame, the bracket of experience Syberberg invests with thought, is the proscenium arch whose method of thinking the film's epic form criticizes. "Performance" is the ironic comment on itself, the close-up (conversely, realistic acting sets everything in perspective).

The operatic is becoming more dominant in the American theatre—in the work of Lee Breuer, Richard Foreman, Philip Glass, Meredith Monk, Robert Wilson, Robert Ashley. It is used to explore past and recent history, but the means of analysis is the theatricalized behavior of the individual in so far as it evolves imagery. (Syberberg is also close to this style because his films are so much like theatre.) So, the theatrical in these examples has two languages: the German, based on behavior and language; the American, generated by imagery.

Avant-garde theatre experiments in general reflect the movement from ritual (the ideals of community) to process (individual technique), from cultural anthropology to personal mythology, from dramatization to documentation, text to image, the public realm to the private, from the chant (group) to the monologue (solo performer) and, finally, from construction to deconstruction.

the life of a style

The Theatre of the Ridiculous is a fascinating case study of how the aesthetics of modernist art can be assimilated in mainstream culture. Originally, the Ridiculous was conceived as a theatre that made fun of and challenged the taboos and values of culture. In its quotation of "high" and "low" forms of art, it developed an iconographical/literary montage style built on the inversion of romantic and heroic images that sustain Western culture. The Ridiculous demythologized myth. But what first was a critique of the cultural mainstream later became part of it.

When American culture itself started mocking heroics and leaning more toward parodying itself in a never ending sense of spectacle that turned everyone into a potential performer, what previously gave birth to the Ridiculous now set the stage for its death. One didn't have to go to the theatre to see the Ridiculous. It was all around us: in theatricalized rock, in the tacky glamour of Bette Midler, in the popularity of Andy Warhol-kitsch, in television's *Gong Show*, then later in punk aesthetics, in the young film audiences who costumed themselves to see the *Rocky Horror Show*, in the flamboyant mingling of the art and fashion worlds as porno chic. Looking back, one can see the beginnings of new wave attitudes in the Ridiculous.

When American culture became perfectly "ridiculous"—undermining political, sexual, psychological and cultural categories in a widely-accepted move toward "liberation"—the "Theatre of the Ridiculous" became hopelessly obsolete (though in its attitude toward the text Mabou Mines seems to have taken over its project as a second generation, refunctioned Ridiculous). "Bad" or "dumb" or "ugly" art have been accepted as aesthetic categories. In the metaphysical burlesque of popular culture, life is beginning to look more like art.

Of Tourists and Refugees, Joseph Chaikin's most recent group piece, Schechner writes: "the problem with this work is that it isn't new. And what was exciting in 1965 is a cold omelet fifteen years later." He makes himself sound like a culinary theatre gourmand who has taken one too many bites into the belief that the artist must always invent something "new." What the "tradition of the new" Schechner espouses should mean, realistically, is the continual emergence of *other* artists who are experimenting and building on what came before them.

Take Beckett as an example—one can speak of a "Beckettian tradition" but has the writer himself done anything "new" in the last decade or so? No—but Thomas Bernhard, one of the many who came after him, has reinvented "Beckettian" writing. One has to distinguish between *self-parody* and *style*. In criticizing Chaikin is Schechner criticizing Open Theatre acting as a cliché of sixties performance ideas, or as a style?

Perhaps it all has to do with the sociology of taste. Chaikin's delicate sentiment seems out of fashion in today's theatre which values self-conscious, ironic art, the raw, the overtly personal, an overflow of contradictory imagery, technological expertise—his work seems too simple, undercooked. If Chaikin is trying to discover what each moment *feels* like, others are more interested in what each moment *looks* like. What separates Chaikin, and Schechner, too, from most of the other directors/groups working today is that he stages symbolic moments, others stage metaphors, in work that generates emotional content more than imagery.

With the increasing lack of influence of these two directors, the emphasis on the anthropological/social as a model of experience leaves the main current of avant-garde theatre. Conversely, Mabou Mines exemplifies the contemporary movement of theatre from myth to metaphor, from the universal to the cliché, emblem to image, acting to performing. The transition is from theatre about life to theatre about theatre. I think we've lost something important—moral seriousness—and gained something questionable—cynicism—in the shift.

the self as text

What I miss in solo performance is the sense of a "world" in the performance space. (Not "the world" but any world.) The audience has to accept the viewpoint of the performer/creator in this totally apolitical form that doesn't acknowledge contradictions (it has no objectivity). It prefers to outline "reality" entirely within the contours of subjective consciousness.

Spalding Gray's solo work is the most prominent example of an artist's refusal to make connections about the life he observes. He will not exert himself *to think* about what he sees, he simply documents his reality in a continual process of unmasking that plays off the roles he creates in his group projects. The solo performance (monologue) describes reality while theatre (dialogue) analyzes reality.

In Gray's solos one simply listens, not having to think about anything. The audience is deprived of a mediating consciousness that transforms raw experience into a new equation between the artist (self) and the world (other). I see in

Gray's work the despair of an actor who has given up his belief in doing "great" art (playing remarkable roles). His solos are the work of someone who no longer wants to do theatre, but to "do" life.

In *Camera Lucida,* the last book he wrote before he died, Roland Barthes described the relationship between Theatre and Death: to act is "to designate oneself as a body simultaneously living and dead. . . ." Of all the artists who responded to Schechner it is Spalding Gray who speaks, metaphysically, of Death in the same breath as *presence.* He is the most religious of performers: while others concern themselves with survival, he longs for salvation.

There is a strain of *performance* (not *acting* which is about pretending to be someone else) that extends all the way from vaudeville to the Ridiculous to the current avant-garde theatre: the performer who expresses an attitude about the activity as it is occurring. The performer "comments" on the action as himself/herself, not as a role-player.

This "performance" tendency runs all through American theatre as a counter-thread to the Stanislavsky-Strasberg school of acting which emphasizes that the actor is pretending to be someone else. Acting plays the illusion while per-formance presents an "attitude" toward illusion.

In hindsight, the emergence of the solo performer seems the inevitable outgrowth of the continuing emphasis on the performer's freedom to be himself/herself in the theatre situation.

All art is life but all life is not art. The predominance of autobiography in per-formance has already begun to show its limitations as a theatrical genre. The erosion of the boundaries between the public and private self subverts the con-ventional dynamic of behavior and thought in theatre, but having done that it doesn't make the personal any more memorable once the story of the self becomes too familiar.

The personal experience has come to be overvalued in the theatrical repertoire which is not a natural home for it anyway. And, in an odd twist it sabotages new literary theory by forcing one to understand the work in terms of its author's life. Instead, interpretation should move away from the study of the author and toward understanding the *world* of the work.

LeCompte writes: "the most radical development in theatre was the combining of the playwright, director and designer in one person." This "radical develop-ment," aside from being untrue historically, is simply an example of the avant-garde's extravagant claims for the individual artistic imagination. If anything, that holy trinity-in-one God-view is demonstrating more and more the exhaustion of ideas in an avant-garde theatre that keeps quoting itself.

another look at "the author as producer"

In Brecht's epic theatre, Walter Benjamin found the example for his theory about turning spectators/readers into producers (as opposed to consumers) who would change consciousness by challenging the political/social order (the means of production). At first the avant-garde theatre's acceptance of the audience as "collaborators" in the theatrical experience—collaborators in the sense that they made room in the theatre experience for the individual imagination to assert itself—seemed a radical step forward from the original theory, even an elaboration of it. Clearly, it opposed the institutionalized thinking in traditional theatre.

This opportunity for the audience to think theatre through without being presented with a closed value system, or order, seems less and less true as the author's/group's point of view disappears in the theatre. Because imagery is often too ambiguous, too available, and finally, technologically in advance of human capacity to assimilate it in a *critical* way, audiences are again being turned into "consumers"—consumers of imagery that is more seductive than challenging to the intellect. (When people talk about a theatre experience now, they tend to talk about the images that impressed them.)

The Brechtian style—the epic form which is *the* contemporary mode of expression—has been too assimilated by an advanced technological media to engender critical thinking. Avant-garde theatre presents no alternative to the image of contemporary culture when it imitates its forms.

[1981]

Performance/Art/Theatre

THE ART WORLD HAS ALWAYS HAD AN AMBIVALENT, EVEN sneering, attitude towards theatre. Just fourteen years ago Michael Fried was proclaiming in *Artforum* that presence, duration, and acknowledgement of the spectator obscured one's perception of the art work because they embraced the theatrical experience. This obsessive purist went so far as to claim that "the success, even the survival, of the arts has come increasingly to depend on their ability to defeat theatre." I think the larger, unarticulated question has finally to do with property: who owns aesthetic space—the spectator or the art work?

Fried's project for saving modernism, now so dated, so High Art-infested in its trembling good intentions, was turned upside down in the last decade when artists embraced both "low art" (as he would have called it) and the theatrical.

Enter Douglas Davis, again in *Artforum*,* writing a "post-performancism" manifesto, telling everyone it's alright to do theatre, to mix high and low art, to be someone other than yourself. "To hell with medium-as-medium, structure-as-structure, New Wave-as-the-next-thing. . . . Let us have instead a reliable verbal umbrella: 'Post-Performancism.' " I wouldn't trust that patchwork umbrella on a rainy opening night.

Wherever he looks Davis finds "performance-film-television-radio, sourced in the popular as well as the visual arts." He's like Molière's upwardly mobile "bourgeois gentilhomme" (Davis is fond of alluding to Molière in his article)

---

*This essay was written in reaction to an article on "Post-Performancism," which Douglas Davis published in *Artforum*, October 1981.

who is startled to learn that he has been speaking prose all his life. In Davis's recognition scene he discovers that the arts influence and feed into each other, and that the theatrical, in particular, absorbs all temporal arts.

Davis is not alone in his sudden acceptance of an expanded notion of performance. The art world in general has little by little become more accepting of theatrical experience. It was inevitable that this should happen because art and art theory cannot sustain artists' prolonged inquiries into the nature of performance and audience. Likewise, as performance art moves toward theatre, dance moves toward narration and emotional content, painting toward representation, the installation toward setting, photography toward drama, and theatre toward opera. The arts are becoming more involved in the exploration of time and narration, after many years of an obsession with space. The mistake of the art world was to believe in the first place that performance is an *art* form when in fact it is a *theatrical* form with its own set of imperatives. One cannot circumscribe performance within modernist doctrine which, as Davis relates, denounced revivalism and objectified all phenomena (surface-as-surface, self-as-self). The theatrical impulse lives its own aesthetic cycle outside of faddish art talk. And if "performance art" is to have an ongoing life, it will have to be saved by theatre. I think many artists and critics now realize this.

Performances have been referred to as "sculpture action," "events," "actions," "happenings," "non-static art," and "art performance," among other things. Everything but theatre. Artists have always exhibited an anti-theatrical impulse, from the classical avant-garde movements of dada, futurism, et al., up to the present. Even in the last decade or so, the visual artists have moved closer to performance while trying to avoid theatre. They haven't fully taken into account the elements inherent in using a form that evolves in time and before an audience, a form that is not about the use of materials, auto-biography, or getting out of the gallery system, as artists have wrongly supposed. And they've ignored the matter of skill which theatre is based on. If artists accept anything as "performance" then anyone can be a performance artist, but not everyone can be in the theatre because every "act" is not theatrical.

Davis's article, one of a growing list of inane pieces on performance that *Artforum* is known for publishing, demonstrates to what extent art critics, in this case Davis, lack a theatrical vocabulary and theoretical base. Besides being ignorant about theatre—he mentions no contemporary theatre work—Davis's ideas are so old-fashioned they predate Stanislavsky. His art talk is all veneer: you can see all the cracks just below the surface.

One cannot talk about performance exclusively in relation to art history: Davis writes as if all changes, trends, and preoccupations in performance grow out of an evolving art theory—modernism or late modernism—not out of cultural forces. Of all the arts, theatre is the most sensitive to society because language, gesture, and the performer are central to it, and theatre encompasses every single other art form as it transforms itself through time and history. It is understandable that, in the art world's earliest dealings with performance, writing about the form was naive and shallow, but art critics and artists have now had twenty years of contemporary performance work to study and expand upon, and their ideas about theatrical form are hopelessly unsophisticated.

Finally, when the media has given everyone the possibility of being a performer for a world audience, when the creative expression of self through acting out has been encouraged in all formal expressions of American culture, performance as a human activity—probably the first, most religious, most celebratory of acts—seems less to do with art theory and everything to do with how individual life is lived in the community and in the world.

Individuality was initially preserved through the solo performance; it is a form anyone could use because it is totally self-centered. But in the long run, the solo performance form leads to a dead end because it is based exclusively on the personal experience, and with that as the sole resource, one can hardly expect it to be more than a brief phase, even exercise, in the life of an artist. Solo performance cannot create a "world" in the space as theatre can. And dialogue (theatre) is more complex a way of thinking than the monologue (solo). Performance art tends to talk to art history, theatre to history itself.

Certainly Davis seems unprepared to think deeply about the implications of performance activity for the individual in society, and for audiences, too. He brings up the subject of comedy but the discussion goes nowhere because he has no resources with which to analyze comedy as a form, nor to speculate on why it is a dominant form in performance today. Comedy is not popular simply because we are nostalgic for old movies and TV, or because it's a reaction to the "seriousness" of the modernist stance, as he suggests. Rather, comedy's popularity may have to do with the fact that it is a conservative form, one that celebrates the individual's capacity to endure, to preserve the individual spirit in a universe (even if it's simply the "world" of the performance) of disorder. Unlike tragedy which is based on rebelliousness and longing, comedy is more interested in survival—comedy shows a disinterest in aspirations toward greatness.

What can one do with a critic who states, ". . . we are peculiarly barren in theoretical depth when it comes to issues like parody, reference, comedy, imitation, irony." "We" have no less than two thousand years of writings on these subjects, available to whomever takes the trouble to get to a library or bookstore and do some research. The point is, there is a rich theatrical heritage to draw upon, if only as a starting point.

Davis has so little knowledge about the theatrical experience, and the range of emotions and forms it engenders, that it is not so much a case of his giving the wrong answers about the topics he raises as it is of asking the wrong questions. He mixes up architectural terms such as "direct recall" and "revivalist" when he should be discussing the use of quotation and rehearsal technique. "Rehearsal is the modality of revivalism," he proudly announces. Nonsense:

rehearsal has nothing to do with revivalism, it's an attitude toward performance, a value placed on skill.

Where Davis is most confused is in writing about *performing* which he doesn't
distinguish from acting. (He also should rethink his definitions of originality
and authenticity, imitation and representation.) He uses Michael Kirby's 1965
definition of "non-matrixed" performance—a definition no one in the theatre
except people writing dissertations has used in years—and tries to assert that
"the matrixed actor stands at the center of Post-Performance." First of all, in
the art world there are performers, not actors; secondly, matrixed (to use this
silly term) acting has generally to do with naturalistic acting in a play in which
setting, character, and dialogue contribute to a unified whole. The context of
Davis's manifesto is so ludicrous—he simply doesn't speak a theatrical
language—that one is tempted to believe it's really a comedy act he is writing to
spoof manifestoes.

Davis obviously doesn't see much theatre so his ideas about the forms are
oblivious to twentieth century experiments. When he quotes actors on acting
he quotes Coquelin (1887) and Sarah Bernhardt (1924). If he were writing
about new painting would he quote a nineteenth-century realist painter to
define the form? Finally, why does the art world consistently tolerate mindless
thinking about performance while it upholds standards in writing about visual
art? This kind of writing is both unhealthy and dangerous in its influence on
artists and their public, and on performance itself.

Oh well, what does it all matter to someone who says Post-Performance
"gladly risks recall and thus courts the false charge of imitation. If this be
Neoclassicism, [another case of mistaken identity—Neoclassical theatrical
theory is directly opposed to the hybrid mix of forms Davis embraces] we stand
or fall on that ground." No thanks, I'll sit this one out and, with Coleridge
(another of Davis's quotable notables), suspend my disbelief. Perhaps it's been a
performance all along, with Davis simply acting out a new vision of the comedy
of manners. After all, hasn't he said that in the Post-Performance era it's okay
to be yourself and not yourself?

[1982]

Nuclear Theatre

FOR MONTHS NOW, ALMOST A YEAR, I HAVE BEEN KEEPING a file of clippings under the title "Nuclear Theatre." Into this file I put all the printed references to theatre terminology that increasingly fill reports on new weapons systems, European politics, U.S.-Soviet relations, anti-nuclear protests, arms limitations, and endless related topics. Most discussions are framed in the language of theatrical metaphor whose usage clues us in many ways how language and thought evolve in American culture.

The Department of Defense's *Dictionary of Military and Associated Terms* defines "theatre" as a "geographical area outside the continental United States." In its original Greek (*theatron*) the word "theatre" means "a place for viewing." The "European theatre" then (or "NATO theatre")—I have never encountered anywhere the phrase "American theatre" or "Russian theatre"—is regarded as the predetermined setting ("theatre of deployment") for "theatre" or limited nuclear war, the implication being that we in the U.S. and in Russia are the audience, Europeans the actors, unless "proxy war" erupts and other characters in the nuclear drama take over the roles. Are bombs the props of the "theatre nuclear forces"? The Circular Error Probable has all the stage directions blocked out. There is no mistake about it, the use of the word "theatre" demonstrates how imperial logic seeps into language, but more important, how it contributes to artificial discourse and human behavior.

The very notion of "theatre" or tactical nuclear warfare is linked to the elaborate theory of deterrence which is really a euphemism for the agit prop theatre in which each side engages, the ritualistic word play that purposely confuses intentionality, pretense, and uncertainty. The rhetorical drama that is at the heart of East-West relations is fueled by the role-playing of masked superpower players whose dialogue has a frighteningly improvisational air about it. The thought that nuclear war might be a chance operation is overwhelming.

Yet, this stylized doublespeak goes on, generating new "scenarios" comprised of code words to drive you MAD (Mutual Assured Destruction). The actors in this absurd drama terrorize us with their psychological games devised to upstage one another, this one promising a weapons freeze, that one arms reduction. Quite simply, deterrence theory offers the greatest performance opportunity for its protagonists since it is based largely on acting out the forever changing psychological attitudes toward possible scenarios. Carter's Presidential Directive 59 is one recent example, but another more theatrical one was last November's discussion of a "demonstration" of nuclear weapons—a "dress rehearsal" as it were, for a play that is always in the making but must never be made.

More and more characteristics of Aristotelian tragedy manifest themselves: in the hubris of world leaders, their high-flown rhetoric, their separation from the life of the people, their belief in Necessity. Even the introduction of the term "fratricide" (the destruction of nuclear weapons which fly into the debris of explosions from earlier exploded weapons belonging to the same country or an ally) into the war vocabulary threatens to convert real danger into the familiar thematics of classical drama. (By now we are aware of the "second generation" and "family" of missiles, but this perverted attempt to make weapons a part of the "nuclear" family was underway already with the first A-bomb explosion at Alamogordo when it was telegrammed to President Truman in Potsdam that the "little boy was born.") Domestic drama has always been America's theatrical strong point.

When war strategists appropriate the vocabulary of theatre by linking it to family history, they distort the deeper imagery of human relations. But not by chance has theatre provided the metaphor for war. The most social of art forms, the form in which one experiences the representation of life in a space filled with living bodies, theatre invites *participation*, which is what war psychology when it mobilizes a country is all about.

The kind of imagery rehearsal that is taking place all around us elaborates a profoundly disturbing mode of thinking because it regards history only in terms of spectacle: Europe as a "staging ground." Not only does it abstract war, it aestheticizes war and our feelings towards it to the point of anaesthesia. The feeling for form, the desire to create and control human images in dynamic settings, to construct dialogue, to structure social relations, to manipulate emotions—in short, to create a world on a stage—is a human need for representation that must not be isolated from moral vision.

The growth of the media and communications in the evolution of modern society has turned theatricalism into *the* twentieth-century political/art form: it subsumes both ideology and individuality as our way of being in the contemporary world. The incursion of the media into every realm of experience sabotages the notion of private acts, turning performance into a way of life: the media as public eye has set the private "I" on a world stage. What matters then is the imagery of the event, how it is presented for mass consumption, even seduction, and sometimes protest.

In its most dangerous manifestations theatricality values appearance above essence, accommodation above ethics. Construed in such a way as to ignore human values, a regressive politics of theatrics is founded on the idea that reality can be fabricated entirely through the manipulation of public imagery.

(A more healthy politics of theatrics is represented by anti-nuclear war protesters who use the performance mode to create guerilla theatre actions in marches, their posters and placards generating dialogue and imagery that criticize the war machine. Even more so, protesters who costume and make themselves up as Hiroshima victims, by submerging themselves in death imagery that confronts the horrors of war, regenerate feelings for life in their acting out of the human dimension of war. This conceptualizing of oneself is nothing short of a therapeutic survival tactic.)

Let us not let nuclear war be defined for us as a casual theatrical spectacle, for if we do we shall become like Bernard Shaw's pathetic wartime characters in *Heartbreak House* who praised the sound of bombs overhead for their similarity to Beethoven's music. Let us not welcome nuclearism as the next style in the everchanging theatrics of contemporary politics.

[1982]

Writers II

Pirandello
A Work in Progress

AN EXCURSION TO AGRIGENTO

An oversize unfinished stone slab marks Luigi Pirandello's grave, settled uneasily beneath the shady umbrella of luxurious pine, and cypress elegance, not far from the sea. "I am a son of Caos," wrote the man who asked to be returned here, naked, his body wrapped in a white sheet. No one could bear to throw his ashes to the wind, as he had wanted, so they are buried here, too. His characteristic play on words was an exercise in double entendre, "Caos" being both the name of the place in Agrigento where he was born, grew up and brought his bride, and which in the end would mark his death, and that of a god who gave his name to the troubled state of the universe.

Chaos it is said was first called Janus, the name of the solar god who presided over daybreak, and guarded passageways. He was the two-faced god who could see from any perspective. He could in effect be his own audience; one side of his face reflected and inverted the image of the other, so that the self could watch itself in the act of seeing. Janus, who presided over the coming to light and the act of going inside, and Chaos, in sum his other face, his double identity—light and darkness—unite in mythological coincidence to define the Pirandellian character, a myth for our time.

It would have been difficult for anyone living near the Valley of the Temples that dominate Agrigento not to feel the presence of the gods and their mythologies. Since the sixth century B.C. the temples the Greeks built on a hilltop stage in homage to them have faded into honey-colored ruin before their Sicilian audience. Yes, it would have been difficult to ignore these giants of the mountain who manipulated the fate of the poor puppet mortals who lived on the shaky earth below. The gods are particularly quarrelsome in this part of the world, earthquake country, always coming apart. A landscape unpredictably capable of falling away beneath one's feet, it bears a natural, free relationship to dramatic action.

Agrigento: its Latin roots (*ager*, ground; *gens*, people) define it as a place where people have a special attachment to the land. Perhaps to words as well. But even that is not enough to explain why Pirandello chose the name "Marranca" for a character in one of his early plays. By what act of fate am I an unrealized character in a drama I did not choose to make? Fated, in quintessential Pirandellian style, to live both the past and present of my character. Alas, Marranca—he had only a last name—was merely a judge's functionary: even dramatic names can signify class distinctions. (Perhaps that is why the Marrancas came to America.)

Here I sit, Pirandello at my side, dreaming in his plays that so timelessly color the landscape of drama, so many ruins to wander through, in search of the future. Will the servant act the master, and I now play the judge?

Here I am, writing about Pirandello who wrote about Marranca. He knew what a "Marranca" was because he found a name for it. The fictional character lived in his world, and in his imagination. Now Pirandello lives in my world. A fiction in the play of my imagining. I shall have my Pirandello, as he had his Marranca.

PIRANDELLO, A WRITER

Pirandello has become a forgotten author in American theatre even as his theories on role-playing are so spectacularly realized today in American culture. Lacking a strong tradition of critical discourse on dramatic writing, American criticism tends to link the history of theatre to the history of production rather than dramatic literature. Not surprisingly, Pirandello has been remembered more for his vision as a man of the theatre than as a writer. Yet, he is one of the most original writers the world of letters has ever produced, and perhaps it is only looking backwards from the perspective of contemporary literary ideas that it becomes apparent how he had anticipated, debated, and dramatized the most radical of them half a century ago. Pirandello was always a deconstructionist, not even stopping first to go through a semiotic phase. He could not waste his time being caught up in a closed scientific system of codes. He rejected the tyranny of the sign as an illusion of those who wished to construct the world. He wanted to break it apart. He was interested in the way the world was perceived by others, not in the way it saw itself. Pirandello only created structures for the paradoxical purpose of destroying them. In superb logic he used reason to show how reason itself couldn't be trusted in the comprehension of reality. Indeed there was no reality, that is, no fixed form one could call Reality, only an elaboration of texts of possible realities: reality as endless fiction. Pirandello's obsessive creation of the open text of the world was simply a mask of his own obsession with death, the last word in the life one writes in the world. Pirandello, who did not love life, loved death less. It was the ultimate lifeless form. His constant reference to art (that is, writing) as birth was another way for him to feel he was resisting death.

Who has thought more complexly about writing, the interaction of fiction and the real, the conventions of theatre, its public, its critics, the act of interpretation, the burden of celebrity? (Before long those literary revisionists, the post-modernists, will be claiming him as an exemplary writer, but he will frame them in a prism of Pirandellian irony by showing up the incestuous crossbreeding of modernism and post-modernism.)

Who has been a more self-conscious, self-critical writer than Pirandello whose plays, essays, stories and novels question, contradict, and intrude upon one another? He rewrote his stories in dramatic form, and parts of his essays he put in the mouths of dramatic characters. It was inevitable that this writer who throughout his life theorized on the subject of form and its promise of fluidity, would turn eventually to drama because only this form, among all the strategies of writing, finds new life every time it is transferred from the pages of a book to the bodies of live actors in a theatre. Moreover, he highlighted the difference between the text and the production by creating at times elaborate stage directions meant only to be read. No two actors would ever say, "We bring you a drama, sir" in quite the same way, and so the dramatic text would forever embody the possibilities of transformation. Pirandello forced the very subjects of drama and theatre—representation, dialogue, acting, presence, and audience—to make a philosophical account of themselves, even creating an entire trilogy to explore the reality of representing fiction on a stage. Years before the concept of the "intertext" was popularized by literary critics he was putting fragments of one text into another, and even more splendidly, in the plays he constructed both real and fictional versions of himself that would first generate the myth of Pirandellism, then turn around and demythologize it.

Play/Writing

1.   What usually happens in theatre is that characters act out a story that moves from a beginning to an end. Pirandello's characters, however, tell a story about an event that happened prior to the play, while at

the same time acting out the event of the play, which is another story. Frequently, a character is haunted or manipulated by a scenario from his past which is just as much a part of the conception of the character as the present. The past (his own or someone else's) the character is forced to confront is always only a fragment: either the text is never completed, or there are so many characters offering so many conflicting texts or points of view that what actually happened can never be authenticated (the question of authenticity is linked to the accretion of fictions, not lies). This collision of texts is the catalyst for the dramatic action. (*Right You Are*)

2.   The text inside the text creates a situation in which there are two stories, and two sets of characters, evolving simultaneously, and in relation to each other. The texts interrogate each other. (*Each in His Own Way, Tonight We Improvise*)

3.   The collective creation: a group of characters agree to believe in and act out a fiction which is socially convenient for them, the rules of the game the characters follow determined by group consent. Other characters, sometimes those who even helped to create it, try to break through this fiction to uncover the "truth," or to erase the "fiction" that has been transformed into "reality." (*Henry IV, The Pleasure of Honesty, Cap and Bells*)

4.   A character/writer attempts to construct a fiction from a real life situation, in a special synthesis of fact, fiction, and imagination. The writer then becomes trapped in the separate levels of the story he is attempting to write. (*To Clothe the Naked*)

5.   Some characters have no "reality." Their lives consist of the search for a fiction to live (*As You Desire Me*). A character may also have too strong an identity which he tries to shed and take a fictional one instead. (*When Someone is Somebody, The Late Mattia Pascal*)

6.   One group of characters brings a text to another group for the purpose of producing it before them. (*Six Characters in Search of an Author, The Giants of the Mountain*)

7.   Characters are always trapped in a text—not a Freudian, psychological text of the unconscious, but one that evolves (or doesn't) in social life —that is, publicly, not privately. There is no unconscious world in Pirandello's characters, only material existence. His characters, with the exception of the raisonneurs and those aware of the game aspect of

role-playing, have no inner life, only an external, social one.

8.   Pirandello had his characters act out his own obsessions with writing: they were given the problem of creating a text in almost all of the plays. He even devised a model of the relationship between the writer and his critics: the author or authors of a text come into conflict with a character or group of characters who criticize and evaluate the probabilities of the text.

9.   Pirandello the novelist and Pirandello the dramatist found a radical synthesis in the dramatic form: a text that could exist in two realms, one narrative, the other dramatic. This tension of genres allows for the possibility of experiencing the plays from the perspectives of both fictional time (the past of the text being composed) and real time (the dramatization of how these two texts come together in the theatre).

10.   The plays embrace the ideal of the open, unfinished text, an ideal clearly demonstrated in the theatre trilogy, and manifested more poetically in the final, generous irony that Pirandello left his last play, *The Giants of the Mountain*, unfinished at the time of his death. Whatever is known of his plans for it comes from his son Stefano's account. ("He said to me, smiling: 'There is a large Saracen olive tree in the middle of the stage; with this tree I have solved everything.' ") What can Pirandello's return to Sicily for an image tell us about the relationship of the geography of a writer's spirit to his creation of myth? The opening he left in this text is an extraordinary invitation to a director or writer bold enough to extend the original text into a new rhetorical setting that might suggest new myths about the theatrical experience to add to Pirandello's own which stopped with the mysterious words, "I'm afraid! I'm afraid!" It is important to start from that moment of fear, and not to hide the dialogue of the two texts (even to add a third, the reconstruction of the final act by Pirandello's son), but to celebrate the event as subject of a new play of interpretation.

THE MIRROR

Pirandello's characters live their lives in the continuous play of reflecting mirrors: in the eyes that reflect one character's image of another, in the eyes that illuminate public opinion, in the public eye that creates celebrity and defines the rules of social conduct. When characters look each other in the eyes it is for the purpose of watching themselves watch the others who watch them, in the same light that outlines the interplay of public imagery. Analyzed from another perspective, it is the influence of hypnotic suggestion on the individual ego that Freud linked to the development of group psychology. The mirror is another version of the proscenium which frames the dialogue of the "other" in the theatre of humankind: it throws back to the audience a picture of itself. The flattening of the image in a mirror makes the individual like art, an object of contemplation. At the same time it demonstrates the difference between life and art, opens the way to the abyss, documents death, links the present to the past in the act of memory, and even plays the trick of throwing up the image of what is behind the viewer, in his future. On the mirror the text of a life is written in the lines of the face, a unique visual language that only the audience of the eye can read.

The eyes are the reflecting liquid pools of the narcissist, Pirandello's fool mesmerized by his own image. And Echo, the narcissist's companion, plays her part as the quoter of others' opinions, unable to form her own. Such is the fate of the man hopelessly trapped in the worship of his public image, and his friend trapped by the cliché. One concept cannot exist without the other: when there is no self but an image, speech functions merely as quotation. (The development of technology, added to both the rise of the narcissistic personality as a character type and the preponderance of the cliché in mass society, might neatly unite in a forceful analytical statement, if one were to use video and prerecorded voices in a new staging of the Pirandellian obsession with identity and selfhood.) Early on Pirandello pointed to the linkage of the theatrical self and the psychology of narcissism which helps to define the contemporary character.

In the plays themselves one structure mirrors another, the outer drama encircling the inner story, grotesquely distorting it, the conventions of one text set in conflict with those of another, as Delia Morello the character distorts the "reality" of Delia Moreno the person, and Pirandello the author of the play caricatures Pirandello the celebrity, in yet another comic scene.

There is one other figurative use of the mirror, the most exalted one, consciousness, where thought contemplates itself. Consciousness is, ultimately, the subject of Pirandello's work and his most profound inquiries. The act of thinking finds its way to the blank page, a writer's persistent and personal mirror of interrogation and abstraction.

THE MASK

The mask is a linguistic concept, each mask a surface on which an individual writes the text he will present to the world. Beyond the mask, moving inward, is the mask he constructs for himself. The interaction of the public and private

masks creates the struggle for textual supremacy, and finally, the difference between personhood and persona. Pirandello's plays move between the conflicting actions of masking and unmasking: even Signora Ponza's veil acts as a kind
of mask, a blank screen upon which the community projects its own scenario.
Sometimes a character will lift his own mask, to let it be known that he is
watching himself in a chosen role. Such is the wise character who knows he is a
performer. More often than not a character is caught, unknowing, in his own
performance. One type of performance is comic, the other tragic, and together
they approach the condition of the grotesque that Pirandello called
"transcendental farce." They unite in the metaphor of the human being as a
puppet figure manipulated by socially acceptable rules of behavior, an idea
which demonstrates the natural linkage of the puppet and the mask in the
modern concept of character, and by extension, the individual in society.

Pirandello's instructions upon his death:

> No announcements or invitations to the funeral. . . . Let me be wrapped
> naked in a winding sheet. . . . Burn me. And as soon as my body has
> been burnt the ashes must be thrown to the winds, for I want nothing,
> not even my ashes, to remain.

Even in death Pirandello found a way to return to an obsessive idea; the win-
ding sheet was to be a total body mask, impenetrably blank, unwritten on. He
had nothing to say to the world.

SUBVERSIVE ACTS

Though Pirandello incorporated in his writing the genres of symbolism,
melodrama, realism and the well-made play, he did everything he could to
subvert their conventions. He used symbolism's bizarre lighting effects, its ap-
paritions, and interest in the occult, the emphasis on subjectivity and attention
to objects, to analyze the theatrical interplay of appearance, illusion and imagination. He ignored the psychological aspects of the style, while retaining its
dichotomy between inner and outer worlds of experience. More interesting is
Pirandello's attitude toward the individual symbol. One could not expect him
to believe in the interior, hidden poetry of objects, he only valued the exterior
reality manifested in their objecthood which he could then question. He needed the physical presence of the object, to propose the denial of it, and to show
how meaning was absent from it. Indeed, with revolutionary insight Pirandello
denied fixed meaning not simply to the text, but to the world itself. His was
always a negative dialectics. (Pirandello was never attracted to the drama of unconscious or subconscious states of mind—consciousness was his all-consuming
subject—so he was unmoved by the influence of surrealism which, besides rejec-

ting rational thought, and distorting reality, denigrated language, for Pirandello the supreme act of mind.)

Approaching drama from another perspective, Pirandello created melodramatic frames to encircle his plays, then scoffed at the moralism of the genre, proving dramatically that there was no such thing as morality, only contingent moralities. He acknowledged none of melodrama's sexual rules, putting in their place the incest, adultery, and unfulfilled passion that quivered beneath the surface of hypocrisy. And from realism he destabilized the center of gravity which propped up the bourgeois character, and cut away its positivist logic to exalt his own pessimism and lack of faith in progress, and disavowal of objectivity, using realism's belief in the access to truth and knowledge to point out the philosophical differences between thought and action, and the deceptiveness of truthful representation. Much of his criticism was directed towards realistic acting which pretended to create a "reality" for a character (that a "character" could contain reality while at the same time being clearly engaged in artifice was questionable), even forcing an individual to duplicate the existence of another. As *Six Characters in Search of an Author* demonstrated, there was a great difference between the persons of a drama and that drama's actors.

Pirandello also belittled realism's reliance on the use of objects which it inherited from the well-made play, by refusing to bestow on them any narrative privileges. Within the narrative itself he created characters who didn't know themselves, much less let others reveal them, perverting in this way the "recognition scene" of drama—how could identity be determined for certain? If realism presented the closed text, with all its problems resolved and tidied up at the end, the furniture and characters in place, Pirandello purposely celebrated the open-ended situations he created, leaving more than a few plays to find their own endings, on occasion even setting up a scene he would decide not to stage. The theatre he envisioned drew its energy from the freedom of collapsing genres and patterns of thinking, in the text that always interrupts itself to go off in new directions. It was inevitable that Pirandello would be drawn into a struggle with the very form of theatre, a form based on the act of duplicating identity, which he loathed on principle—theatre, confident in its role as a mirror of society, a mirror he distorted ruthlessly. He demolished realism's "fourth wall" with great élan, by bringing real life into theatre, and taking theatre out of the auditorium, an act which anticipated Happenings' invitation to the spectators and actors to co-mingle in the same space. And finally, he created a model for real people to see fictionalized versions of themselves on stage, a development which would refer later, not to the history or documentary play, but to the use of autobiography in the theatre.

Pirandello never stopped playing with and questioning the conventions of making theatre and making a text. He transvalued the old forms in radical modernist settings that encompass theatre and a critique of theatre, drama and a new textuality. Even more importantly, starting with the split between art and life—for the sake of illusion—that characterized realism, and instead highlighting their coming together that defines modernism, he showed how easily the two could be considered variations on the same theme.

SCISSORS

Madame Pace materializes with such an odd character-prop, a pair of scissors. The traditional Freudian approach is to view *Six Characters in Search of an Author* in thematic, symbolic terms. In that scheme of things the scissors are identified as an instrument of castration. The psychological approach, all too common in dramatic criticism, especially on Pirandello, stifles a play in its reduction of it to a series of simple equations corresponding to what is already known, not what can be imagined. On the other hand, a more metaphorical approach to the scissors as an object opens up its poetic options within the world of the play. Metaphorically, then, let's suppose that the scissors cause a tearing apart, a gap in the continuity of the text. With scissors Madame Pace cuts herself an entrance into the text which then has to be pieced (peaced) together again. A director who wants to link new literary theory to the play might stage it as a text about writing, and Madame Pace would signal a disruption, a coming apart of the text; in another setting, perhaps one of political oppression, the same Madame Pace and her scissors might be read as an instrument of censorship.

Every time *Six Characters* is opened to the page where Madame Pace enters the text, there she will be with her scissors hanging from a chain at her waist. But those scissors don't embody meaning. Possibilities for interpretation of a text are a cultural and historical matter. Theatre defines itself as the reinterpretation of the text, so theatre, more than any other art form which has a literary manifestation, embraces the idea of playing with a text, even cutting it apart. A play is, therefore, always in the making. Pirandello's own view of the text as immutable form is romantic, possessive; it encourages the idea of the singular reading. But a text lives only in its ability to change, to give the appearance of having new qualities—it does not exist independently of an historical moment. A "classic" is only interesting when one reads the future in it: anything that can be thought will at some moment be present in the world. Criticism in the broadest sense, whether the work of the director, of the spectator, of the reader, is the activity in which one uncovers the shape of history in a text.

PERFORMANCE ACTS:
PIRANDELLO AND THE ANTHROPOLOGISTS

The conventional anthropological view of performance as social drama, which Erving Goffman, Richard Schechner and Victor Turner have popularized, and linked to theatrical theory, presupposes a belief in a social order that gives all human activity a ritual frame (a predetermined narrative, as it were), as if performance acts were entirely structured by social relations. In contrast to this conservative view of performance (role-playing) as symbolic, the more anarchic mind of Pirandello, who should not be overlooked for his contribution to this area of thinking, considered performance an ontological act, outside the time frame, possessing the power to generate a radical individualism in a performer's gestures toward re-creation. So, while the anthropological school believes in everyday "performances" as a development in the construction of a self, Pirandello, who refused to acknowledge the notion of a "self," more precisely saw such developments as the construction of a mask.

There are two fundamentally opposite views outlined in the directions these two schools of thinking follow, and ultimately, they address questions of politics and methodology. The anthropological view enforces a closed system of signs and structures that define and codify body language and social interaction; this approach, derived from structural anthropology, presupposes a universality in nature. Pirandello's work projects a disbelief in the ability of signs to generate meaning out of context; his view of the world is rather an argument against the fixity of nature as a set of values in a culture. A significant difference between Pirandello's aesthetic definition of performance and the anthropological one, and thus problematically a struggle between theatre and social science, frames the more provocative question: is performance an art or an activity? Anthropologists tend to separate the realms of art and life, viewing performance, which is an aesthetic transformation of the self, as a temporary excursion into art. Pirandello's own thinking moved toward bringing art into life on a more permanent basis, art wasn't simply a way to bracket everyday activities. Art was a model for a more poetic way of life. In light of the current movement of culture, it seems that Pirandello's work offers the more enlightened model for a way of being in the world.

Pirandello makes it clear when a role is *objectively* real to the social order and *subjectively* real to the character. He questions the reality of the parts people play, while anthropologists accept them at face value. Therefore, it is not surprising that Pirandello understood how role-playing isolates the individual in society through the process of aestheticizing experience, by abstracting the individual from his possibilities of selfhood, while anthropologists naively believe in it as a model of the social integration of an individual. Pirandello created three kinds of performers who can serve as prototypes of the individual in relation to the modern problem of identity:

1. the self-conscious performer who watches himself act out society's version of a social role. He abstracts himself to play the *form* of the role, in full comprehension of its cognitive and philosophical dimensions. (Henry IV)

2. the non-conscious performer who has no self-knowledge, only a repertoire of masks. He acts out the *content* of the social role, its informational aspects. (The Unknown Woman of *As You Desire Me*)

3. the performer who is in search of a role to give form to his life. (Ersilia Drei of *To Clothe the Naked*)

The anthropological conception of a role is essentially undramatic because there is no conflict and contradiction between performer, role, and scenario, only a catalogue of images—there is nothing going on beneath the mask to produce a real drama. The socially ritualized performer is no risk to his society, instead he acts out its values. Actual dramatic form, on the other hand, poses a greater danger in its potential for attacking the values of a society, and disrupting its social organization.

Pirandello created a drama that outlines a new relationship between subject (the individual) and object (the world). In its most lavish moments it pointed to the possibilities of individual revolt against established social structures, looking to the freedom of the artist as an ideal. In Pirandello's hierarchy of being "art is the kingdom of perfected creation. . . . Each of us is seeking to create himself and his own life with those very faculties of the spirit that the poet employs in creating his work of art. . . ." And in its cynical moments his drama outlined the individual's capitulation to the crowd. Through the infinite suggestions of irony and its relationship to audience, Pirandello had his masked men and women move between the opposing poles of tragedy and comedy (which special triangle do comedy, survival and performance intersect in?), each with its own set of social imperatives. Now that the social sciences have shown their limitation in creating a profile of the performing self, it is time to recover performance theory from science and return it to a more humanistic study in the reflection of art and morality.

Pirandello's writing opens up role analysis to its political dimensions, a field of inquiry anthropology and sociology ignore. What is the relationship between role-playing and society? How far can one take the freedom to act out versions of the self? What one can add to Pirandello's profound inquiries, and certainly to the social sciences, is an *ethics of performance*, and its necessary adjunct, a theory of performance value. This could be the beginning of a deeper, more engaged perspective on performance in relation to private and public life, self and role, structure and free expression, ethics and contingency, individualism and group psychology.

PIRANDELLO/PHOTOGRAPHY/FILM

Pirandello's thinking is so much a part of the history of modernism it is easy to overlook the fact that he lived thirty-three years in the nineteenth century. How he must have hated that century's invention, photography, for its power to fix reality in the contours of an ambiguous image. Just as he would later use film and the record player (he would have found a way to use holograms if they existed in his lifetime), he turned first to the photograph in order to subvert its relationship to the photographic subject. Hidden in his work is an argument against photography; the camera lens is another version of the distorting mirror. Without literally addressing the topic Pirandello framed the modern problem created by photography and the impulse to reproduce reality: the contradictory relationship between an individual's attraction to images and his alienation from them, and the ease with which the image can free itself of moral and ethical content in its denial of *presence*. That there is hardly any metaphoric use of visual images in the plays (aside from his progressive interest in light and color as he worked more in the theatre) only serves to force his characters to reveal themselves in the way that they are present to each other at every moment. It was inevitable that Pirandello's philosophical insights into the problem of existence would play themselves out in the world of theatre because only this art form acknowledges the "real" value of its subjects while at the same time calling into question the "fiction" of illusion and representation. Pirandello needed theatrical realism, a genre which grew side by side with the development of photography, to criticize the social construction of reality which he viewed as fiction.

More remarkably, in his 1916 novel *Shoot!: The Notebooks of Serafino Gubbio, Cinematograph Operator* which, according to film theorist Yvette Biro, gave to literature its first filmmaker, Pirandello understood from the start the alienation of the cameraman from his machine, " . . . as I turn the handle, I am what I am supposed to be, that is to say perfectly impassive. . . . A hand that turns the handle." As Walter Benjamin, most certainly a writer who learned from this novel, has written, Pirandello also pointed out the alienation of actors in exile from their bodies in the filmic image. It was the loneliness created by the distance between self and role. An artist who revered the liberating act of imagination, Pirandello questioned whether technology as a means of production could be rightly considered an art, and if so, what the role of the poet would be in a "mechanical birth" that separated the act of creation from the creator. Beyond that he connected technology (the camera) and the *consumption* of imagery ("It eats everything, whatever stupidity they may set before it") in a metaphoric thought that describes the way images proliferate in, then dominate, a technological society, prophesying, finally, that life would become like the movies to audiences who would measure life against film reality. The representation of reality would substitute for the experience of it.

Pirandello, who answered so many of the questions social psychology has hardly begun, with few exceptions, to ask could see from the perspective of the inchoate film industry the role mass society would play in a technological age. He sums up his vision at the end of the novel when the cameraman, mesmerized by a growing horror, cannot stop himself from shooting a scene in which two actors are accidentally killed, one devoured by a tiger, the other "shot" by a rifle. As the tiger feeds on the man, the film feeds on him. Now the public will feed on the images, and the film studio on their voyeurism. The final touch of irony is the cameraman's muteness, caused by the shock of witnessing the graphic violence. Now he is a silent film character, merged with his machine. Pirandello's range of critical thinking, in whatever areas of questioning he extended thought, made an original contribution to our understanding of the individual and the loss of individuality in the development of the modern world. Against the backdrop of contemporary society, his insights into the relation of the self to the world of public imagery now appear extraordinary in their visionary provocation.

As with many events in Pirandello's life, he switched sides of an issue when it suited his purposes. If he argued against the encroachment of film as a further division of the individual from the things of his world, he also allowed films to be made from his work, even participating in their adaptation for the cinema. Perhaps there is a clue to his attitude toward film imagery in the choice of two major works which made it to film, the play *As You Desire Me* and the novel *The Late Mattia Pascal*, each of whose central character is subsumed by an identity crisis. In fact, the action of each story is that character's performance in a role he or she creates, then plays, involving other characters in the "fictional" scenario. Film reality was simply another level of illusion, another space in which to depict the philosophical dimensions of his life-long study of the phenomenology of being.

PIRANDELLO IN AMERICA: A VERY BRIEF HISTORY

While most of the American theatre was earnestly engaged in bringing psychological truth and objective reality to the stage, a small countertradition was quietly working to show that there was no such thing as reality in the theatre. The first group of experimenters was The Living Theatre who produced Pirandello's *Tonight We Improvise* and Jack Gelber's Pirandellian play *The Connection*, and on their own reordered reality and subjectivity in a radical vision of politics. But it was eventually to fall to Richard Foreman to take up what Pirandello claimed as his accomplishment, the conversion of "intellect into passion," in his attempts to stage the activity of critical thinking, and just as surely as the actors drove Dr. Hinkfuss out of the theatre, so one of his own creations, the character Rhoda, pushed Foreman aside, having become independent of her Author. Though only on a theoretical basis, Pirandello had anticipated the removal of the author from the theatre by the director, then the removal of the director by the actors, and finally, he went so far as to show the murder of actors by the audience (a juncture to which we have happily not arrived in anything other than metaphoric terms). Mabou Mines carries Pirandello's spirit into another area of experimentation, the ironic interplay of appearance and reality in the social construct of the individual; the actor and the role were further detached in the activity of "performance," which played with the illusion, as opposed to acting which merely reinforced it. Squat came from Hungary with its own surreal political expansion of Pirandellian ideas which would mirror the erasure of the public and private worlds through the looking glass.

But no group has extended Pirandello's ideas (many as yet unexplored even today) more than the Wooster Group (it's no surprise that they eventually gravitated toward Thornton Wilder, America's first Pirandellian), which made the very relationship between fiction and autobiography, and character and actor, the starting point of its experiments. Here the actor himself, not simply the role he plays, is the stuff of fiction. Is it any wonder then that Spalding Gray, the source of the group's major fictions (or realities, whichever way you look at it), should emerge as the consummate Pirandellian actor—the complete (con)fusion of character/actor and real/fictional aspects in one persona? Gray plays out the Pirandellian process to its logical end: he unmasks himself in the solo work, masks himself in the group pieces. He generates myths about himself, then demystifies them. He is the dialectical actor/individual *par excellence*, a true character in search of an author. Gray begins to approach tragic proportions the more he becomes inseparable from the mask, the more naively he lets the audience define his proportions of self and role. That much of his audience now refuses to acknowledge the fictional aspects of his "character" points to the diminishing returns of playing with fiction, and a certain entrapment in reality that poses an intriguing theatrical problem. Having come this far in exposing the realities of making theatre, theatre might now turn around and show how illusions are created there. Perhaps it is time for the emphasis to shift away from the myth of the playwright or director or actor to the audience, and the actual experience of theatre.

PIRANDELLO/BRECHT/PERFORMANCE

In the evolution from acting to performance which, in the world of representation, is the difference between creating illusion and commenting on illusion (representation vs. the real), Pirandello and Brecht laid the groundwork for reordering the relationship between character and role. Pirandello led the way in the separation of the actor from the role (in his theatre trilogy especially), repudiating acting styles of his day which fused the two. What he instigated, and Brecht evolved further though in another direction, was the idea of drama as a critique of reality, from the point of view of the actor. What united them intellectually, and produced this new vision of theatre which worked itself out in the definition of character, was the dialectical method of thinking, a process of thought which ushered in the modern era. The approach to drama as a critique of reality, philosophical in its grounding, has had few practitioners in the twentieth century, but those who brought philosophy into the theatre, to the names Pirandello and Brecht one can add Artaud and Witkiewicz and, in our own time, Heiner Müller, who in his remarkable plays provides the synthesis of Pirandello and Brecht (by way of Genet), have been the most important thinkers in the art. The philosophical drama they created (Artaud excepted because his contributions lay elsewhere than in dramatic form) evolves from a materialist approach to drama, working itself out in the actual production of the text, that is, in the working out of the relationship of character, role, and text, in the theatre event. By leaving room for the character to critique himself and his role in a specific attitude visible in the performing of that role, Pirandello and Brecht instigated the evolution toward "performance": the performer, now demonstrating his separate identity, relinquishes his equation to a character, to act out *his own* attitude toward his contribution in the making of the text; in contemporary performance, he is free to act himself out. (The concept of *performance*, a major development in acting theory in this century, is closely linked to the use of narrative, story-telling, even literary prose passages in the drama. Some breakdown of conventional dialogue, as the completely outer-directed "I" of each speaker, has to occur to allow for a character to move out of a role, and either into himself or into the quotation of a character type or attitude, but more significantly, into a third person-oriented mode of speech presentation.)

The philosophic ideal in drama demands a character who is in a high state of consciousness at all times. The actor, like the character, must be aware of himself in the making of the persona and its relation to the process of making theatre, at every moment. If the character could give a critique of the "character" as written in the drama, so the actor could give a critique of the role in the making of the play. In other words, instead of simply acting his role unquestioningly, the actor/character would have a social attitude toward his status as an agent of reality; he would acknowledge performance as an act. This kind of performance attitude presupposes a new view of audience perception: it led Brecht to the alienation effect, for Pirandello it related to the concept of *humorismo*, the precursor of *Verfremdungseffekt*. Each of these important theories is linked to the role of irony and to the function of the sign in the theatre. Together the two provide the necessary components in the historical progression from acting to performance, which had to wait for the new vision of the thinking actor in the theatre, and the attraction to quotation in society, fully to materialize.

Both Pirandello and Brecht decomposed characters in order to expose their oppositions and contradictions: Brecht studied character in relation to epistemology, Pirandello emphasized ontology. Brecht believed in the wholeness of a character whose contradictions were incorrect political choices—simply the wrong side of the self, false consciousness. Pirandello's characters have no self, no right or wrong side, only an ever-changing set of beliefs contingent on each new situation. If Brecht's characters could learn from experience and change, Pirandello's could not: personal survival was all that counted. The very separate, often dissimilar, research into character that these two writers carried out would lead them to diametrically opposed political conclusions. In one sense, they outline the main currents of political choice at its most extreme ends. These choices evolve from the situation of the individual in relation to the group: Pirandello saw the group and the power of public opinion to maintain psychological control over the individual as a force that deprived him of any individualistic thought or action; Brecht took this relationship but set it in the context of political ideology to show how the group reflected the Marxist ideal of the collective mind.

The crucial difference between Pirandello and Brecht, and thus between different schools of thought on perception, rests with the concept of the mask. For Brecht there was no difference between outer appearances and consciousness because there was no sense of mask. He believed totally in the sign which is the basis for his theory of *gestus*; the creation of a classical mind, *gestus* is founded on the universality of action and truth. Conversely, Pirandello disrupted the logic of the sign, which is the center of identity, because he was only interested in showing up the ambiguity of the signifier, and its inability to sustain a hierarchy of values and identifiable concepts. That Brecht was an ideologue, and Pirandello unsystematic as a thinker, explains their contrasting views on the problem of the sign and its function in society. Pirandello's vision allowed for the concept of the mask to transform itself throughout the twentieth century into the social idea of the image, and because his work relentlessly pursued the elusive meaning of the sign, while Brecht was more concerned with engendering meaning in it, Pirandello is the more important contemporary mind, yet to be exhausted as an inspiration for his observations on social activity.

AN EXCURSION TO PALERMO

A bookshop. Marranca and Bookseller.

—*Do you have any books by Pirandello?*
—Yes, just a moment . . . here they are.
—*An autographed novel, signed 1937. . . . Didn't Pirandello die in 1936?*
—No, he died in 1937.

(Is this a forgery or a European four, I thought?)

SIX CHARACTERS AND THE DEATH OF THE AUTHOR

For Pirandello the text was irrevocably bound up with the primal, instinctual will to survive. In *Six Characters in Search of an Author* which is, at its core, a play about writing, about authorship, major power struggles are played out in a contest of textual supremacy that functions on at least three separate, but inter-related, levels of dramatic action:

1. The text of the characters challenges the text of the actors. A third text, *The Rules of the Game*, a Pirandello play which the actors are rehearsing, intervenes as a reference point.

2. The written text claims hegemony over the unfinished, unwritten, spoken text presented by the actors. "Just because there is no 'book' which contains us, you refuse to believe. . . ." The Father accuses the director and actors, suggesting an argument for the work-in-progress vs. the text already made. Beyond that, it is a rejection of logo-centrism.

3. A conflict arises between The Father's text that forces itself on the other characters and the actors, and The Son's text which he himself refuses to elaborate. In a larger perspective, this generational conflict is part of the rebellion of a writer who offers a breakthrough of new writing to conventional theatre, against the six characters who represent the old melodramas that keep theatre from entering the modern age. The clash of the two views of the text generates a dialogue on the nature of theatre.

What Pirandello does is to show his disdain for stereotypical characters and their text, and the acting company's own stale approach to staging, while simultaneously exploiting them to explore the making of drama in a self-conscious, subversive way that highlights his own thinking about writing for the theatre.

Pirandello valued the life of drama, making it equal to the life outside of art, even more honored than life itself which, he believed, lacked the beauty of form. He had his own theory of origins, which the wondrously passionate sentiment expressed in these lines of The Father describes: " . . . one is born to life in many forms, in many shapes, as tree, or as stone, as water, as butterfly, or as woman. So one may also be born a character in a play." For Pirandello there was a difference between a writer's actual creation (craft) of a character, and a character's natural birth, free of the writer and his technology. Yet, while the characters had life, they did not have a structure.

Some of the questions Pirandello asked in his play that literally did change the "rules of the game," in so far as theatre was concerned, and with great sophistication deconstructed theatre before there was a name for what he was doing, are very simple yet they rush into the soul of writing, and its hermeneutics, in a profound, unsettling way. Who is the author of a text? Can a text be known? Does it embody a fixed, single meaning? Is there such a thing as an original? What is the relationship between the world of the playwright and the world of his characters? Pirandello's six characters call into question the very status of the text, and its transformation in the act of staging which is always, or should be, a critique of the text. They do not doubt that there is a difference between dramatic literature and theatre. The play itself transvalues the relationships of dramatic text/writer/actors as it struggles, theoretically, to find its own life as an autonomous entity—to give itself—going so far as to suggest a concept which in literary theory has come to be referred to as the "Death of the Author," while it continues its homage to the world in the text.

Pirandello was still fighting with the myth of the Author, and the ambiguous pleasures of authorship, toward the end of his career, with his attraction-repulsion pattern creating the paradoxical center of his attitudes toward writing and working in the theatre. But the subject shifted perspective between the time he wrote Six Characters (1921) and When Someone is Somebody (1933), written the year before he won the Nobel Prize for Literature. It moved from the subject of authorship to that of celebrity. Now a famous author invents another identity for himself in the fictional double of a young poet. If in his first investigation of writing there were six characters in search of an author, in his last there is one character who runs away from an author.

In almost everything he wrote, Pirandello studied the relationship of the private and public aspects of an event, finally taking the point of view of the writer in this prophetic meditation on celebrity. Though he complained all his life of being misunderstood or ignored—even when it wasn't so—Pirandello nevertheless rejected more fiercely the status of a "somebody" second guessed by his public. He saw the life of the text as separate from its creator's life, denying the classical notion of individual genius which rigidly joined the two. He saw a public that demanded a writer to live up to its preconceptions of him and his work, denying him the opportunity for surprise and novelty. Eventually his rights would be consigned to the state of "public domain," and he would become a part of history. In his own lifetime Pirandello saw his name transformed from a noun to an adjective, often to characterize work he himself took no part in. When this occurs a man is no longer simply a writer but takes on instead the mythic stature of Author.

When Someone is Somebody is a look at the writer in relation to his public, at the very least an acknowledgement of the media's role in creating celebrity. Pirandello anticipated the link celebrity-making would forge with technology in the play's Nam June Paik-style image of the cliché the famous author, XXX (Pirandello didn't even give him a name), visualizes: "Split my back open and put the gramophone in my belly. Then I'll talk and you can all stand around and listen." Ignoring the privilege of speech, the author commits poetic suicide at the end of the play, actually turning into stone; he becomes a literary monument. "When one is *somebody*, then at the opportune moment, one must decree one's own death and remain locked up, mounting guard against one's self." The public craving for the cult of the author is the end of spontaneous writing: is it any wonder that the rise in global communications has contributed further to this crisis in the world of literature, while at the same time spawning its utopian corrective, the desire for the Death of the Author? Pirandello gave to the world of letters a blueprint for this theory, decades before its need was proclaimed. He had wanted simply to roam in the world of his imagination: to be a man, a writer.

PIRANDELLO IN THE FUTURE TENSE

Pirandello's contribution to the theory of social psychology—the study of the individual in relation to the group, which forms the basis for any social theory of character the work suggests—has been systematically overlooked in favor of what they might reveal about the disintegration of the ego, loss of identity, and abnormal psychology in the individual. His interests extending beyond individual psychology, Pirandello dramatized the loss of self and the breakdown of a fixed social order that made individuality less acceptable, and the power of the group to define thought and action, more attractive. He concentrated less on the psychology of the crowd than on the individual who was ripe for being seduced by crowd opinion. In other words, Pirandello was interested to a lesser extent in the mass mind than in the individual who could be transformed into the mass, through peer group pressure; he demonstrated how this development turned the individual into a performer of roles in the social world, and finally, how performance is related to the concept of the mask in the theatricalization of everyday life.

Pirandello's characters, who change their beliefs from one moment to the next, when confronted with the possibility of isolation from majority opinion, are the ancestors of the unthinking individual in mass society. The plays dramatize people's need for public acceptance of majority opinion, and their inability to cope with the reorganization of social and moral codes, reflecting the historical period of modernism they grew out of. Pirandello understood how society, miniaturized in his plentiful communities of neighbors and family, was shaped by the forces of public opinion: an individual can be influenced by the opinions of others even when they contradict his own rational thought and self-interest. There was no such thing as objective reality, reality was subjective, temporary, infinitely malleable according to the needs of the ruling ethos which defined the uniqueness of individual (that is, separate) realities, and proposed instead that the same values and beliefs be mass reproduced throughout the community. In the writing there is almost always the attempt by characters to control, con-struct, or reshape reality; essentially, he was not interested in the negative energy of disintegration of structures of reality. Looking backward through history it seems as if Pirandello, with the strength of a great writer who sums up the vision of his age, had early on outlined the profile of the individual ripe for totalitarianism, a politics that works through group psychology and the renun-ciation of individualism in a new vision of reality.

Pirandello's plays suggest a social model that reveals the psychological laws of the modern character. His raisonneur, director or author functions as "leader" of the crowd or community, and manipulator of the individual who is set in a struggle with the will of the group. (Interestingly, the pioneering sociologist Gabriel de Tarde first pointed out the link between the role of opinion in small communities and the role of the chorus in Greek tragedy, a relationship which has some bearing on the social and dramatic structure of the plays.)

Pirandello showed that role-playing, the retreat behind the mask, was an act of self-creation, sometimes of liberation, that had the power to turn one into a work of art. He anticipated that the artist, in the age of lost individualism that characterizes modern life, would be the person most able to cling to individuali-ty and independence as mass society valued those qualities less and less, and that the ordinary individual, understanding this gradual loss of selfhood, of poetry, would try to imitate the artist's ability to regenerate himself through

art. Only art holds the promise of transformation and change, but more importantly, transcendence. Art, always in flux, offers a way to keep life from becoming fixed form whose ultimate manifestation is, of course, death. This merging
of the common man with the yearnings of the artist, the desire for art to be
more a part of life, would in our own time, particularly in America, link modernism and its worship of subjectivity to mass culture values, in a new development of group psychology within democracy. Furthermore, the need for
transformation and transcendence, the constant renewal in the act of becoming a new person, is a desperate refusal of death: here Pirandello's life-long fear
of death, and the denial of death which is part of the American experience,
meet in a special ordering of Romantic idealism.

Pirandello showed that role-playing and acts of self-creation (performance acts)
would allow one to create any amount of new images of oneself, in effect, to rewrite one's life, but looked at from another perspective, the liberated individual
who is unable to break through his own subjectivity is fated to recast himself in
the image of what is socially sanctioned behavior and opinion. Pirandello's
masked performers who have no strong inner self—the opposite of realism's
complete bourgeois character, they are like Peer Gynt's onion which reveals a
new layer as each successive old one is peeled away—experience existence purely from the outside. They thrive on their need for a public persona within the
public realm (the public eye). The plays demonstrate the disappearance of the
private realm, the prologue to the totalitarian process, and the emergence of
the public realm as sole mediator of opinion and belief. In the public realm one
can only be a performer of sorts, playing an assortment of roles currently in
fashion, because it is unsafe to be seen without a mask. The private I is expendable—maintaining an acceptable image is all that counts. ("Image" is simply a
contemporary revisioning of the concept of the mask, a more visual metaphor
that suits a technological age.) Finally, Pirandello's ubiquitous mirror, in this
context, gains deeper metaphoric significance as the symbolization of public
response (the audience) to the individual act.

The contemporary infatuation with performance as a way of presenting oneself
in public, and totalitarianism, which has always been linked to spectacle, imagery, the creation of fictions, and theatricalized public life, intersect at this
juncture. (One of the early modern social psychologists, Gustave Le Bon, connected crowd psychology to the role and power of images in public life, a relationship which is becoming more and more discernible with the assistance of
technology and its influence on mass mentality.) Pirandello, who was not a
political artist, followed his aesthetics all the way into fascism, unable in the
end to separate art and life. Will the contemporary attraction to the aesthetic
way of life, the gradual submersion of individualism in group ethos, and the
disinterest in maintaining a distinction between public and private lives, in-

teract to create the social conditions ripe for totalitarianism, or will they more kindly show that democracy and totalitarianism, two different approaches to illusion, are at the same time two possibilities of the same desire for transcendence?

[1983]

Reading Chekhov

Dear Dimitry Vasilyevich [Grigorovich]!
[. . .] If I possess a talent worthy of respect, I humbly confess to you who have a pure heart that up to now I have not shown it any respect. I felt I had talent, but had fallen into the habit of considering it insignificant. [. . .] All those close to me have always treated my writing condescendingly and never stopped advising me in a friendly fashion not to give up my true profession for mere scribbling. I have hundreds of friends in Moscow alone, among whom are twenty or more writers, and I cannot recall a single one of them who would read me or consider me an artist. [. . .] During the five years I've spent going from one newspaper office to another, I adopted the prevailing opinion about my own literary insignificance, and quickly started to regard my literary endeavors condescendingly, and yet I kept writing! That is the first factor. The second is that I am a doctor and up to my ears in medicine, and I think that the old saying about chasing two hares at the same time has never deprived anyone of more sleep than it has me.

I am writing all this in an attempt to justify to some degree my grave shortcoming in your eyes. Until now my attitude toward my literary work has been frivolous, negligent and casual in the extreme. I cannot recall a single story of mine that I spent more than a day writing, and actually "The Huntsman," which you liked, I wrote in a bathhouse! [. . .]

I cannot put my real name on the book because it is too late; the cover design is ready and the book already printed. Even before you said so, many people from Petersburg advised me not to ruin the book with a pen name, but I did not follow their advice, probably out of pride. I do not like the book in the least. It is a mishmash, an unshapely batch of scribblings from my student days, picked clean by the censors and editors of humor periodicals. I believe that many people will be disappointed after reading it. Had I known that people were reading what I wrote and that you were following my literary development, I would not have agreed to let the book be published. All my hope is for the future. I am only 26 years old. Perhaps I shall still succeed in ac-

complishing something, although time is flying. [. . .]
Please believe in the sincerity of your deeply respectful and grateful

A. Chekhov

CHEKHOV'S VOICE

His writing is remarkable for all that is absent from it, the tension between the spoken and unspoken, the scenes of drama left unplayed, the unfinished characters, the interrupted gestures, broken sentences, and half thoughts. What draws one into it are the events not complete scenes, the tiny explosions, disruptions, and irregularities of moments, the glimpses of an act. Chekhov's writing has the ambiguous, soft lines of exquisite watercolors that quote no more than the shapes of things. His fiction highlights an extraordinary intensity in the audacity of its disinterest in telling all of a story. In his drama he loves to leave stories unfinished, to begin stories about characters who never appear, and to narrate off-stage events, this masterliness proving that the incorporation of fictional technique in theatrical form expands the drama, revising the concept of dramatic time, and its constituent, dramatic action. Chekhov brings a new sense of time into drama: the time of silence, desire, the emptiness of characters who "sit silently, deep in thought." Paradoxically, the fullness of each work is bound to its quality of incompleteness. Absences are what convey the restless feeling of loss at the center of the writing.

Chekhov does not overstrain his voice, nor does his writing shout. A modest man, he does not overburden the reader/audience with the Voice of the Author. So much of the narration, then, is carried freely in non-verbal yet semantic space (in the landscape, in objects, in sound). These are the sensual spaces that comprise the world of appearances, surfaces whose simplicity is so disarming they are easily overlooked. In his writing Chekhov celebrates the worldliness of all things, their freedom of speech, and in doing so develops a narrativity shared by people and the inanimate, even space, as equal forms of life. In the theatre experience he honors the idea of objecthood as the basis of theatrical dialogue, in the broadest sense of the term.

Because Chekhov speaks less in his plays, the characters speak more, bringing a wonderful naturalness into the acts of stage speech: characters actually seem to be talking, not speaking writing. Sometimes the talking verges on singing and the characters beg to be cast in musical form: why hasn't Chekhov been transformed into opera? They tell about themselves, endlessly, unable not to communicate, even if dialogue seems often a parenthetical remark addressed to no one in particular. The truth is they love company: whoever is present is drawn into their emotional opulence and transient moods. The dramatic characters have a unique way of communicating with each other, in random comments, asides, non sequiturs, and sudden outbursts of feeling, and communicate they do, because this is really how people talk among themselves —half listening, now answering, now ignoring bits of conversation. The sequential speech of conventional drama, its attachment to causality, seems stiff and artificial next to actual speech.

Chekhov gave drama its first characters organized around acts of speech that imitate *talking* and the simultaneity of activity and speech that define the conversational experience. It does not matter even if no one replies to these incessant talkers: what counts is the act of speech, the words, their power to evolve a language of dreams in the company of illusion. This world is made up of language. Yet, the characters don't have a name for their emotional state and can only describe its symptoms as they search for a text that will create their lives. It is seductive, this dreamy life lived in the subjunctive mood, which is why Chekhov's writing is so sultry, sensual. His characters live in the erotic state of desire, the realm of unfulfilled passion. Is it not natural that they should so often hear the sound of string instruments which more than any other embody desire's tone?

They are so open in describing the physiology of their feelings, it seems as if we know their bodies too, and this great emotive longing generates an overwhelming intimacy in the theatrical experience. The palpable reality of their presence induces the author's disappearance, his withdrawal into another corner of the drama. This absence opens up the text, freeing it from fixed ideas and interpretations, flabby psychologizing, single-minded theses and morality, the quintessence of Ibsenism that Chekhov disliked. Instead he situated the making of the drama in the distinct speech styles of each character, and this symphony of voices precludes the possibility of a single tone of voice, especially the author's, dominating the conversation. Words, words, and more words echo past the arches of the large rooms the characters wander through in search of a little drama in their lives.

As a body of work the writing, not only the plays, clings to the idea of theatricality by acknowledging the role of the reader/audience in the act of composition. "When I write I rely fully on the reader, assuming that he will add the subjective elements to the story," wrote Chekhov. Unfortunately, critics in his own time and throughout the twentieth century have misread the interplay of subjectivity and objectivity in his writing, and so ignored its strong sense of engagement.

In his responsiveness to the personal point of view Chekhov leaves room for others to imagine aspects of a character not present in the text. A generous writer, he does not keep all the adjectives and images for himself: if his plays emphasize the act of seeing, the fiction tests powers of observation. He leaves the reader space to wander in the language. For well over one hundred years experiments in fiction that emphasize the phenomenal, and his stories are part of this line, have made the relationship of reader to text more flexible, yet his plays by virtue of their being part of the more conservative world of theatre, still startle audiences by their ellipses.

The Chekhovian sense of freedom comes from a real lightness and vulnerability, yet a lack of fear of not knowing the why of an action. In this refusal to seek answers, and simply to propose the questions, lies a rejection of power that writing can claim as its privilege. So many critics have underestimated the strength of his style, the ironic loveliness and understatement, the slow deliberate rhythms, the thoughtfulness so supremely elegant. Instead Chekhov has been turned into a tearful, sentimental poet because he does not fit the stereotype of a "masculine" writer. He left the role of the patriarch, Russia's conscience, to his friend Tolstoy: "When literature has a Tolstoy, it is easy to be a writer. Even if you are aware that you have never accomplished anything and are still not accomplishing anything, you don't feel so bad, because Tolstoy accomplishes enough for everyone." Chekhov himself prefers not to judge nor to set moral standards, he makes no grand gestures; a miniaturist, he scrutinizes life's simple moments; he is gentle, unpossessive, lacking in self-importance; his writing is graceful, he has a womanliness in his hands. The quality of androgyny we have only lately come to appreciate in him and in other "soft" writers (Barthes, Kleist) who render ineffectual preconceptions of the body of the writer in the writing. Sometimes it seems as if Chekhov wrote with a piece of thread instead of a pen. Perhaps his writing is sewn, and only appears to have been written.

Chekhov's manner of speech apparently confuses those who deride him, even if unknowingly, as an "objective" or "neutral" writer, those who say he has no politics, no firm social vision, no social program. Such critics need to hear the Voice of the Author, they cannot hear writing itself. But Chekhov diagnosed his own "autobiographobia": he would not put his private life into his work in a pretentious way. He would not speak for his writing. Yet, he was not silent.

What, then, is "political" in writing? How does writing speak? Surely, it must be in the ideology of longing in language, it must be in the landscape of an imagined world, it must be in the models of human life that theatre, the most dangerous art form, presents as probabilities in their possibility of being acted, it must be in the body of writing: its repetitions, contradictions, imagination, eccentricities, sensuality, silences, joys. In vain readers search for meaning behind the text when the meaning of writing, in the truest sense, is always on the surface, in front of it, in its future.

The example of Chekhov embarrasses most definitions of "political" and "social" aspects of writing expounded in critical discourse. Together his life and work demonstrate why political thinking, that is, the worldliness of personal expression, is a question of taste, a feeling for form. Indeed, in the nature of its expressivity the writing itself outlines why writing is always a political act of the imagination, politics being the condition that makes a human being worldly.

In his sublime worldliness Chekhov did not aestheticize his political feelings, he acted them out. A doctor by training, he was also engaged in grass roots affairs at almost every community level—health, education, science, culture, transportation—helping to build schools, libraries, roads, museums, bridges, clinics, hospitals. He turned his exhaustive census of the brutal penal colony at Russia's Far Eastern borders into *The Island: A Journey to Sakhalin*, a book which provoked changes in the country's prison system. One would have extensively to search throughout world literature to find a writer in whom social vision and art are so seamlessly manifested. And yet, there are those who persist in writing about Chekhov's lack of social engagement, his neutrality, his simple interest in human experience. The subject of politics has always shared an unhappy alliance with art in the world of critical discourse, as if the two could be separated. Critics have degraded Chekhov's reputation: thinking they were praising him, they were instead burying him in empty rhetoric. The blindness of such critical thinking takes the life out of art, political feelings out of both, and leaves neither the art nor life, merely a repertoire of clichés that carry from generation to generation until the artist too disappears, and all that remains is the utilitarian Babel of loud, institutionalized voices.

FEMINISM / MODERNISM / HUMANISM

In the works of Chekhov feminism and humanism are inseparably bound as an ethics. He wrote female characters from the point of view of their own, rather than male, psychology. He understood sexuality as an expression of womanhood. This unwillingness to disenfranchise the minds and bodies of women for fictional purposes allowed women to lead their own lives in his writing. His refusal of such power freed them from bearing the burden of moral example. Chekhov created fascinating independent women; there were others who had no will of their own; they were successes and failures; capable and incapable of change. But the important point is that they existed in the world on their own terms, with their own special longing. They were simply a part of the larger idea of freedom that made Chekhov the great, free man that he was.

Virtually alone among the artists of his own day and in the years that quickly followed, those artists who would create modernism, from the turn-of-the-century till World War II (encompassing symbolism, *Jugendstil*, expressionism, early absurdism, futurism, dadaism, surrealism), Chekhov acknowledged women, free from hierarchy, in the grand design of life. Because he was that rare modernist who extolled the future of humankind, he could accept the biological role of women in the order of nature, yet not sentimentalize it. And because he rejoiced in the female body for its participation in the creation of future worlds, he could acknowledge the totality of womanhood in all its palpable fleshiness. He was an anomaly among modernists, for no modernist movement honored the ordinariness of daily life and its material complexities, and even more so were women's bodies dishonored as they, the agents of birth, were equated with the social diseases of bourgeois life that modernism projected onto them, in literature and in art. In the modernist revolt Woman, as mother and organizer of family life, was appropriated as a symbol of cultural malaise and corruption. Contrary to this view, Chekhov's modernism subsumed feminism in a comprehensive humanism. He respected the female body for its own sake, an attitude which precluded any conception of it as a repository of vulgar bourgeois values. For him Woman was not a scapegoat or social pariah.

The example of Chekhov proves why feminism and humanism must be integrated in any responsible world view. Deeply political in its imagination, humanism is a philosophy of life that determines the choices one makes to behave, to work, to take pleasure, to socialize, to die; it determines one's gestures, and perceptions of art, social issues, ethics. When in *Uncle Vanya* Chekhov links what seems exclusively an issue for women to large socio-political ones, the totality of his viewpoint grows frankly insistent. Yeliena says to Vanya: "Why can't you look at a woman with indifference unless she's yours? . . . You spare neither woods, nor birds, nor women, nor one another." The issues of acquisitiveness, territoriality, and domination are brought together to measure their relationship to women, the environment, animal life, social affairs. In the Chekhovian landscape all things have a right to their own life. What Yeliena addresses is the subject of violence, in all its guises, specifically how violence is contained in the little gestures and thoughts that comprise daily life. Her outburst orients itself within the broadest social context: feminism and humanism are united in the conjugation of the verb *to be* in the order of decency and equality.

Vienna
March 20, 1891

My Czech friends [the Chekhov family],

[. . .] If you only knew how lovely Vienna is! It cannot be compared to any city I have seen in my entire life. The streets are broad and elegantly paved, there are so many boulevards and squares, the houses are six or seven storeys high and the shops—they are not shops, but sheer vertigo, dreams! The windows alone display millions of neckties! What exquisite articles made of bronze, porcelain, and leather! The churches are enormous, but their immensity is not overpowering, they caress the eyes because they seem to be spun out of lace. St. Stephen's Cathedral and the Votiv-Kirche are especially beautiful. They are not buildings, but petits fours. The Parliament, the Town Hall, the University are truly magnificent. Everything is magnificent and it was only yesterday and today that I finally realized architecture is an art. [. . .] Every little side street has its own bookshop. Some of them even display Russian books in their windows, but, alas! they are not by Albov, Barantsevich, and Chekhov, but by all sorts of anonymous writers who write and publish abroad. [. . .]

Imagine, ye of little faith, what the cabs are like here, devil take them! They have no droshkies, but brand-new handsome carriages drawn by one or often two horses. The horses are wonderful. The coachman's seat is occupied by dandies in jackets and top hats, reading newspapers. Courtesy and service.

The meals are first rate. There is no vodka, people drink beer and wine that's not half bad. One thing, though, is annoying: you have to pay for the bread served with meals. When they bring you your check, you are asked, "Wieviel Brötchen?" that is, how many rolls did you gobble down? And they charge you for every single roll that you've eaten.

The women are beautiful and elegant. In general, everything is devilishly elegant. [. . .]

I am homesick and miss all of you; besides, I have a guilty conscience for having abandoned you again. But it is not so terrible. When I get back, I won't stir from home for a whole year. Regards to everyone! [. . .]

I wish you all the best. Don't forget this miserable sinner. My humble regards to all, I embrace you, bless you, and remain

Your loving,
A. Chekhov

THE IDEA OF PERFORMANCE

Chekhov's approach to the problem of identity situates itself in his idea of performance as an attitude toward perfection. Living itself is a performance act, but more than that a question of ethics: to live fully one must do all in one's power, in all endeavors, to honor the act of being. Performance is inseparable from the overriding Chekhovian law of work; as one must work in the outside world, so must one work inside oneself to strive to be a finer human being, and help to make a more humane world for those who will follow. In this context, then, the performance act does not derive from a repertoire of superficial roles that fluctuate according to contingency rules; rather it has ontological urgency as the evolving life process of social engagement, a way of acting in the world that defines an individual's all-consuming center of existence. This act is both theatrical and ethical, a matter of self respect and respect for others. The self is always in the process of becoming an ideal self that watches and critiques its own movement toward perfection. This is what it means to live life as a work-in-progress. The idea of performance is embodied in the apprehension of consciousness as a theatrical act: through consciousness one is both subject and object, actor and audience. There is a second, larger audience, society, in which the self projects itself as it wants to be known to the world.

Chekhov's own life was a magnificent performance. This son of a serf obliterated the slave in himself to become a gentleman, a humanitarian, a free thinker, a graceful soul, an artist in the truest sense. He led an exemplary life that in its longing for perfection evolved into a work of art.

In the writing there are many characters, men and women, who reflect an urgent desire to redefine themselves. Some fail, others succeed in their new roles: that is always a matter of individual strength and need. The most complete portrait of a character who remakes himself is that of the young aristocrat who becomes a house painter in "My Life." His performance as a worker, the self he reconceives as a protest against the indolent life of a rich man of his class, is so thorough that his very structure of feeling becomes "proletarian": an actual, complete worker-self emerges, not a new mask of the same man. "My Life" is the chronicle of a life narrated by its subject: he documents the process of transformation by which certain aspects of a self are erased and others cultivated. Understood in this context, performance as a reconception of the self—the profound consciousness of Being—is a positive act of individualism. In a deeply spiritual sense it is also a search for salvation. That Chekhov gives this possibility of transformation to women as well as men, and to all classes in society, reflects his sophistication in comprehending that the need for transcendence, for personal freedom, indeed the very recognition of it, is not circumscribed by gender or class. Rather, it is a subversive, moral gesture toward perfection.

The earliest of modern drama's solipsistic figures, Chekhov's characters outline the boredom and uselessness of a class displaced by historical time and rendered obsolete. Yet, they are so like the contemporary temperament in seeking self-actualization, purpose, a home in the world—ultimately, an action around which to build their lives. All Chekhovian movement is, ultimately, the search for this comprehensive action: a story to live.

(Chekhov could entertain the idea of performance as an honest, natural act only because of his abiding faith in the world, in the individual will to act, and his great freedom of thought regarding human potential. If he had no hope, if he were a cynic, he would not have thought that a human being could change or that the world could, and finally, that change mattered at all. That he believed in the goal of a unified self, and did not devise fictional worlds in which characters have a repertoire of roles, public and private, accounts for his vision of an open, democratic society in which everyone works for the good of all, with access to the greatest number of possibilities. The Chekhovian ideal is wholeness in the organism. The interchange of public and private roles is only necessary in closed societies which offer no hope of change, or very limited potential for change. The doctor of "Ward No. 6" courts personal disaster in the totalitarian environment of the mental hospital where he works, but he will not act a role to save himself. He has only one self, not many. He refuses the totalitarian prerogative of living both private and public lives. Paradoxically, in such a world one does not choose roles, they are thrust upon one. Totalitarianism and theatricality have a special relationship in the evolution of self because they help to shape the role of illusion in public life.)

There is something in Chekhov that reaches out to the purest, most genuine aspects of upward mobility (and all the euphemisms by which it is known) as social aspiration. The notion of progress was central to his view of history. It was part of his medical training, and influenced his views as a man of letters. That much of Chekhov's energy was spent improving the living circumstances of his family and himself, and neighbors and friends partly explains his social vision in so far as it refers to human transformation. The process by which Chekhov erased the serf in himself led to his becoming bourgeois: the idea of performance, in this context, is fulfilled in the bourgeois ideals of culture, refinement, and respectability as positive social values. For him the change meant discarding consciously many of the values he grew up with and that characterized the first social world he partook of, and choosing others. Chekhov was a self-made man: he created his own way of being alive.

Chekhov invested the landscape with the same goals as he did humans, for nature too was life, not merely its scenic background:

> The sea had roared like that down below when there was no Yalta or Oreanda, it was roaring now, and it would go on roaring as indifferently and hollowly when we are here no more. And in this complete indifference to the life and death of each one of us, there is perhaps hidden the guarantee of our eternal salvation, the never-

ceasing movement of life and earth, the never-ceasing movement towards perfection.

("Lady with Lapdog")

SEEING AND BEING SEEN

Characters frequently catch each other in acts of transgression. There are no secrets in their domestic spaces: everything is observed because the Chekhovian world is the world of experiences. It absorbs all that the eye can see. When the concept of privacy is unacknowledged, characters experience the drama as a group. Konstantin spies on Nina and Trigorin, Anna finds Ivanov with Sasha, Koolyghin watches Masha with Vershinin, Vanya surprises Astrov and Yeliena in an embrace. Those who see are forced to confront illusion, deceits, lies. What is seen is measured against what is unseen. The act of seeing is important because it is related to illusion: seeing is a function of theatre which is perceived wholly in relation to illusion.

Seeing evolves an inner theatricality within dramatic action whereby one character, as audience, watches other characters act between them a "social" drama. The character observing can use the knowledge gained in the act of seeing the others to make a critique of his or her reality, and adjust that reality vis-à-vis illusion. Or, the character can simply choose to ignore the information and enjoy the delusion. Chekhov's drama offers characters the possibility of change, though this option is rarely taken. They don't want to change. They are content to be what they are and let others see them just so. They make no attempt to hide themselves. In fact, their charm is in the courteousness of their expositions. Even the lakes of the Chekhovian landscapes conspire to reflect the characters in their world which seems to be made of glass. It is a measure of the worldliness of things that they should see and be seen: the act of living is realized in the presence of an audience. One of the great pleasures of seeing these plays performed is sharing the act of presence with characters so deceptively present.

The contemporaneity of drama is defined by a character's relation to illusion. The audience experience occurs in a dual level of theatrical reality that the plays propose: seeing the characters in their acts of seeing and their subsequent denial of sight. This is the antithesis of conventional movement in drama in which seeing, that is, knowing, leads to dramatic action. Chekhov's characters have the freedom to do nothing, and this inability to act is the source of their humor, and the prerogative of modernity as well.

THE GEOGRAPHY OF DREAMS

Chekhov's characters have a constant need of movement. This is noted ironically in Masha's (*The Seagull*) wonderful complaint, "I'm trailing my life behind me like a dress with an endless train," all the more laughable in that it alludes to the improbability of her ever going anywhere—by train, boat, or foot. How much walking about and pacing there is in the plays! The restlessness of the characters was paralleled by Chekhov's own wanderlust. Travel was life itself, the future, space an aspect of the phenomenology of desire in him and in his work. For Chekhov there were several trips abroad, the long, dangerous journey to Sakhalin Island, frequent trips between Yalta and Moscow after he was married (his desperate need to finish writing *Three Sisters* and join his actress wife in Moscow entered the fabric of the play itself . . . perhaps if he hadn't made the trip to Moscow, the sisters would have). He would no sooner arrive at his Melikhovo country home than he longed to travel to Europe or back to Moscow, and after he had spent some days there he would be eager to escape again to the country. Travel was the dramatic action of his life. How like this poet of Russian life to be abroad when he died.

Everything about Chekhov's plays—the fiction doesn't have the same desire—announces their need for the feeling of space. In fact, the drama consists precisely in the desire for drama (action), not the action itself. That is why the plays are ruled by the concept of landscape, which refers to space (a future), rather than by the concept of setting which is confined to a past. The dramatic tension in the plays is heightened all the more by the contradiction of seeing immobile characters in a spaciously generous world. Chekhov wrote the most uncluttered, airy plays in the long history of realism, he brought light into realism. Life flows through them like a confident warm breeze. This ideal of space was related to the notion of personal freedom: one could not exist without the other. The longing of the dramatic characters was situated in the country, it was not an urban state of mind. And, it was Russian, not European.

For Chekhov places denoted a special geography of dreams. Europe represented a world of beauty and culture and civilization. He loved Italy where "Art is not looked down upon as in our country" and Vienna because there "you may read anything you like and say whatever you please." (In their blustering way Russian censors understood the lyrical connection between cities and the act of imagination as freedom to travel in one's own thoughts, and so in early editions of Chekhov's letters they cut out passages and omitted letters that praised foreign cities and the western way of life.)

Yet, this geography had its dark side, as did most joy in Chekhovian sightlines.

In Monte Carlo he experienced what he called the "roulette luxury" of gambling and dining that dishonored life, even affecting the landscape forced to host the truffled opulence. "There's something in the air that offends one's sense of decency and cheapens nature, the sound of the waves, the moon," he wrote his brother Mikhail from Nice in 1891.

America had a special poetry which he instinctively related to space as an element of myth. It is to America that Sasha wants to run with her pathetic Hamlet (*Ivanov*), there, too, goes the liberated Masha to see an art exhibit, leaving behind her husband ("My Life"), and in the dreamer Astrov's study there is a divan upholstered in "American cloth." The vast wilderness of Sakhalin made Chekhov compare it to Patagonia and "Texas." He thought of America when he wanted to get away from pressures: "I want to go to America or somewhere still more remote because I have become dreadfully fed up with myself." Alas, he never made it to America though he considered returning to the Russian mainland from Sakhalin by way of the Pacific; the ever money-minded writer decided not to take the American route because he had heard it was too "expensive." Instead he went by way of the Indian Ocean, stopping in Ceylon ("the place where I found paradise") whose "bronze women" added to his sense of geography a greater feeling for latitude. These experiences the same Russian censors also eliminated from the letters. To enjoy the sites of the body is an act of geography just as unmentionable as cosmopolitanism.

———————

Melikhovo
July 13, 1892

Forgive me, most kind Nikolai Alexandrovich [Leykin], for not answering your letter sooner. As a result of the cholera epidemic which has yet to reach us, I have been appointed by the zemstvo as a member of the sanitary corps and assigned my own region, and I am now riding around from village to village and from factory to factory gathering data for a conference of the sanitary corps. I do not have time even to think about literary work. Back in 1848 there was a terrible cholera epidemic in my district; we estimate that this time it will be no less devastating, although of course it will be as God wills. The districts are large so the doctors will spend all their time in exhausting trips from one place to another. There are no barracks; the tragedies will be played out in peasant huts and in the open air. There are no assistants. [. . .] Besides cholera I am expecting another epidemic that will undoubtedly attack my estate. Its name is penury. Once I put aside my literary pursuits, my income was also curtailed. Apart from the three rubles I received today as a fee from a gonorrhea case, my income is exactly nil. The rye was a success on all fourteen dessiatines. It is being harvested. Due to the re-

cent rainfall the oats are doing better. The buckwheat is magnificent. There are loads of cherries. [. . .]

Yours,

A. Chekhov

RE-READING THE PLAYS

Pirandello and Chekhov/*Ivanov*

Chekhov's characters are less than a generation away from those of Pirandello who recognize, even accept, the masks they wear in public life. The Chekhovian character does not yet distinguish between appearances and reality. Yet they are incredibly close to exposing themselves as role players highly conscious of acting out fictions. (Trigorin is trying not to be a performer, but the others force him in that direction.) Ivanov, however, is an exception: he is already looking into the mirror that reflects the modern temperament. Ivanov and the doctor Lvov are proto-Pirandellian characters (so are Astrov in *Uncle Vanya* and Chebutykin in *Three Sisters*). The movement of *Ivanov* is toward its hero's recognition of his self-dramatization, and his eventual unmasking at Lvov's instigation. Ivanov is aware that he is "playing" Hamlet. Unlike the more typical twentieth-century character, however, he refuses the game; he lacks the ironic detachment of the raissoneur, the modern cynic. He is tragic, not comic. "I caught sight of myself in the mirror—and it was like a shell exploding in my conscience. I laughed at myself and nearly went out of my mind with shame."

Ivanov's tragedy is that he is aware of his unrealized "performance" as the new man of Russian liberal society, the man who will change the world through his more progressive thinking and hard work. He cannot name his alienation in the modern sense but he experiences it. This recognition, and the subsequent unmasking, leads to his suicide. Because he has ideals and faith in the world, he cannot live with his failed performance. Chekhov's consideration of the idea of performance in everyday life as a moral attitude, his belief that one can construct a self as a liberating act of consciousness and independent thought, is connected to ethics. Therefore, it is not the same use of role-playing that Pirandello describes in his plays, performance for the purpose of acting faithlessly, as if one were merely playing a game of survival. Suicide for Ivanov is an act of self-respect. Unlike him, the Pirandellian anti-hero does not take his life because he hasn't invested the world with any fullness of meaning or morality. This moral relativism is not an attitude in Chekhov's writing.

Chekhov abandoned the concept of the mask as his drama became more open, and the characters more expressive. He had to let it go because the mask encourages repression of feelings, not their exposition. He did not isolate the individual into public and private selves. Ultimately, he was not interested in the act of role-playing and its inseparable adjunct, the mask. He attached more importance to essences and truths rather than deceptions.

Writing a Play/*The Seagull*

Chekhov's most self-consciously theatrical play, the one whose writing made him say, "I am more convinced than ever that I am not a dramatist," is *The Seagull*. At times it seems solely to be about approaches to writing a play, viewed from at least five different perspectives: 1) the acting out of the drama itself from start to finish; 2) the play-within-the-play; 3) the narration of off-stage events; 4) Trigorin's notes for a story in the making; 5) a line from one of Chekhov's own stories serves as the catalyst for Trigorin and Nina's affair ("If you should ever need my life, then come and take it" from "Neighbors" becomes a passage in one of Trigorin's books). The story of *The Seagull*, then, is the struggle of the many texts which clash in the lives of the characters. The outdoor stage remains in place during the two years the play unfolds as a constant reminder that the characters are attempting to dramatize a story. Which one?

There is Maupassant's *Sur l'eau* which is read aloud and then put aside as "boring." Arkadina and Konstantin play out an improvisational text on the themes of *Hamlet*. Arkadina has her own text in the old plays which she appears in, which determine her idea of theatre and also influence her over-dramatic personality. ("You the last page of my life," she tells Trigorin, as if she were thinking of her life as a work of art, perhaps a novel.) The text of the young writer Konstantin offers the new "decadent" symbolism. Nina fails in her desire to stage her text, the twice repeated section of Konstantin's play. Nonetheless, what dominates the line of the play is Trigorin's own work-in-progress, the text that is in the making: he creates the story of *The Seagull*. At the end of Act Two he outlines it. "A subject for a short story: a young girl, like you, has lived beside a lake from childhood. She loves the lake as a seagull does, and she's happy and free as a seagull. But a man chances to come along, sees her, and having nothing better to do, destroys her, just like this seagull here." The action of *The Seagull* is the development of this text which Trigorin successfully stages, overpowering all the others. Konstantin's attempts on his own life are enacted in despair at his inability to keep this text from being performed. He makes a valiant effort; even at the end of the play his text is still running through Nina's frantic speech.

Landscape and Scenery/*Uncle Vanya*

The difference between Astrov and Serebriakov, the new man of the world and the old man of a dying society, is explained by their approach to nature. What makes Serebriakov such a short-sighted, egotistic fool is that all around him he sees only *scenery* which he regards as decoration, data. "Wonderful scenery," he says upon returning home from his walk. Astrov, on the other hand, understands the concept of *landscape* as a measure of culture and social responsibility. He does not use the word "scenery," he talks of "landscape" or *paysage*. Serebriakov does not see himself inside the landscape: it is outside of him, detached from his way of life, the Other. For Astrov, contemplation of the landscape, apart from ecological awareness, is a measure of how one lives humanely in the world, how one relates to time and to space and to history. In his modesty before nature he grasps the idea of landscape as metaphor, imagery. For Serebriakov the scenery is only pictorial, illustrative; it has no resonance beyond his indifferent consumption of it in a passing glance. Landscape represents a world of history and feeling for Astrov; he makes it, it makes him.

Chekhov, The Squat Theatre and Marguerite Duras/*Three Sisters*

What is missing in productions of Chekhov by American directors is the dark side of the Chekhovian landscape, the languid dissipation, cruelty, decadence and utter desolation of the characters, the banality of their language and gestures, the simmering passion beneath the surface. Most productions here play only the emotions, sentimentality and nostalgia, the silly trilogy of existential denial that comprises the American view of Chekhov and makes his plays excessively theatrical in an old-fashioned way. Completely contrary to this approach the Squat Theatre, in a production of *Three Sisters* originally performed in Budapest in 1976, broke apart the play when they produced it again in New York four years later. Needless to say, it failed miserably with audiences (even their own avant-garde followers) and the press.

Three male actors, dressed in white suits, played Olga, Masha, and Irina, on a small platform containing the barest of furniture. A woman crowded in a promptbox about six feet from the edge of the performance space first spoke the line of dialogue (only the sisters' lines were performed and these only in part) which was carried over a sound system, then repeated by one of the actors. The entire performance, about an hour long, proceeded in this way.

In their eccentric rethinking of *Three Sisters*, Squat went to the heart of the text, taking Chekhov's own wish to de-theatricalize theatre to its extreme ends. Squat emptied the play of its fussy emotions and gesticulation, and flattened the language, turning it into clichés. In the act of men playing women's roles they reversed the emotional identity of the play. By having the prompter first speak the dialogue through a microphone before it was spoken by the actor, Squat brought out the element of quotation in bourgeois language, emphasizing how it echoes through historical time. The echo effect evolved two time structures: the story narrated (on the sound system) and the one enacted (on the platform). The use of the prompter gave each line a past before it had a present in the voice of the actor, and that sense of echo alluded to the meaning of the quotation as cliché. The production concept translated *Three Sisters* into a world made up entirely of language, a static world in search of a new language.

Squat's highly stylized *Three Sisters* situated the entire drama in the voice, always the site of longing in Chekhov's work. In its absorption in speech the production recalls a similar experiment of the same period, Marguerite Duras's play/film *India Song*, in which no characters speak, but the story is narrated on tape as voice-overs of characters confined to a closed space. To see Chekhov done full blown Duras-style would bring a whole new dimension to the work.

Chekhov needs to be recovered in a modernist context that would highlight his affinity to the *nouveau roman*, the icily refined cinema that grew out of it (Duras, Resnais, et al.) and the new realism in contemporary drama and film (in Germany, especially). (*Three Sisters* can be viewed as a prologue to Handke's *The Ride Across Lake Constance*.) American directors have for too long drowned Chekhov in tearful psychology and cluttered settings, too timid to explore the phenomenological yearning in his plays, the worlds of language, therefore, obscuring the extraordinary evocativeness of presence in his theatre.

Dream Play/The Cherry Orchard

ACT ONE

(*A room which used to be the children's bedroom and is still referred to as the "nursery."*)

LOPAKHIN: The train's arrival, thank God. What time is it?
DUNYASHA: It's nearly two. (*Blows out candle.*) It's light already.
LOPAKHIN: How late was the train then? Two hours at least. (*Yawns and stretches.*) How stupid I am! What a fool I've made of myself! Came here on purpose to go to the station and meet them—and then overslept! . . . Dropped off to sleep in the chair. Annoying . . . I wish you'd woken me up.

If one were to stage this scene of *The Cherry Orchard* twice—once at the opening of the play, then again at the end—the whole play can then be reflected as the dream of Lopakhin who has fallen asleep in the nursery before Ranyevskaya and the others arrive.

CHEKHOV AT MELIKHOVO: A FICTION

"Contempt for women as for a lower creature or possession has come to such a pass that the Gilyak does not consider slavery as reprehensible. Strindberg, that famous misogynist, who thought women should be slaves, follows the Gilyak pattern. If he happened to visit northern Sakhalin, they would embrace him warmly." Chekhov laughed and put down his pen. Making fun of the Swedish writer took him out of the sober mood of the book he was writing on the penal colony's inhabitants. More and more humor was creeping into the book, he thought, recalling that he had already written of the old woman who cried bitterly when she told him about her twenty year sentence, then quickly asked, "Won't you buy some sauerkraut?"

He got up out of his chair, walked around his study, through the sitting room, grabbed a piece of fruit from the dining table, hurried down the front stairs and around the house. It was nearly dusk. He hadn't realized how long he had been writing. But he was glad the Sakhalin project was interrupted because he never liked to miss walking in the garden, inspecting all his flowers, trees, and vegetables, this time of day. He was always amazed to see how much things grew even in one day.

The sun threw a pink blanket across the horizon. Already the yellow-green haze had disappeared from the hay field. A warm breeze was making the tops of the trees shimmer like a parasol over his head. Just as he thought he saw a mouse run past him—he had been catching as many as twenty-five a week and carrying them off to the woods—his two dogs ran after him, jumping up to the flaps of his coat pockets which smelled of mushrooms. "Fine race, dogs," he said to the dachshund pair, Bromine and Quinine. Quinine looked even chubbier than she did yesterday, dragging her little stomach along the edge of the field as they walked together, as if she were dusting the ground.

Chekhov circled past his rose garden, beyond a long row of linden trees at the edge of the pond. He was particularly proud of the four dozen red roses he had planted a year ago. They formed twice as many buds as any of his neighbor's roses, and longer stems. The neighbors had laughed at all the trouble he took to prune them in April, with shears he himself had made. Perhaps it was also the sulphur treatments he gave them that made the difference.

Chekhov had his own special remedies for treating plants. After he decided to plan a garden and orchards, he read as much as he could find on gardening, and spent whole days trying out new methods. He subscribed to *The Compleat Gardener* from Germany. He brought back seeds from France, and a copy of

The Garden Architect which Bouvard and Pécuchet had mentioned. He was particularly interested in finding out the latest ideas on hybridizing lilies, and keeping animals away from the fruit trees. Just beyond where he is now standing, he can see the bags of human hair (his sister Masha's) he left hanging from the apple trees to keep the deer away. Once he put a bandage on the broken stem of a cucumber plant.

Walking around the setting he had created for the roses, he came upon a patch of freshly cut hay. He loved its sour smell. Scattered forlornly about the field the bales of hay looked like broken wheels of giant carriages which had rolled off their hinges. "I'm lazy, I ought to get back to my book," he thought to himself as he fell onto the lap of the earth. He gazed up at a sky that did not want to give up the day for night. Shades of blue were still struggling through the pink. A big cloud in the shape of a grand piano sailed past him. He began to hum Chopin. "What an orchard I have!" "What lovely flowers!" he thought, drifting off. He began to picture a play with a group of characters and a lake and lots of love. Then he thought of writing a story about a bishop. He was in the gentle state of mind between sleep and dreams.

Someone sat hiding behind a lilac bush watching Chekhov from the moment he had walked past the side of the house. It is the young writer who has taken the train from Moscow to present his book to Chekhov. Hundreds of writers from all over Russia mail or personally deliver their manuscripts to him for comments. He never refuses any of them. His criticism is honest, to the point. "Your treatment of heroes, for instance, the actors, is old-fashioned." When he saw the tall Chekhov stretched out so peacefully on the hay, staring up into the sky, he suddenly became afraid to approach him. So he just stood there. Chekhov looked as if he did not want to be disturbed. . . .

MONEY

Money is an important issue in the writing. It usually appears in relation to survival and independence. Chekhov did not write about acquisition, consumerism, or commerce, the abstract themes of economics. He wrote about losing money and needing money. Because he supported his family throughout his life, he worried about making money from his writing. He was concerned with what things cost, how much he spent, what he was going to get for a story. Poor as a boy, he grew up to be a man who understood the value of things. The act of writing itself was connected to making money: it was not something he did in his "free time." A man who worked continually, he had no free time. His transformation at twenty-six, from Antosha Chekonte to Anton Chekhov, had to do with his sudden deep comprehension of the value of his work as a writer. The name change signified a new life of the mind, and its worth. Chekhov would no longer squander his gifts. Not after the great writer Grigorovich called him the most talented writer of his generation.

Chekhov's characters always expose their attitude toward money; ironically, that distinguishes their value, their "worth" as social beings, whether they themselves work or live from the labor of others. It is part of the totality of character that makes them who they are. Most of Chekhov's leisured characters simply eat, sleep, read or go for walks; they have nothing else to do with their lives. One of the larger themes in the writing is the moral significance of work as an adjunct of social justice: through work one pays a debt to society for the gift of life. In the Chekhovian order of human existence work establishes the continuity of life and reaffirms its purpose. Part of Vanya's humiliation is that he has worked slavishly and not been properly paid for his efforts. Only when he reinvents for himself the significance of work can he find meaning in his actions.

That the ages of characters is so often given only emphasizes how they have "spent" the years they have lived. Chekhov shows how attitudes toward money and work are joined as indicators of an individual's social awareness. The characters' constant complaints about how old they feel, their laments of lost youth, their hypochondria draw attention to the fact that they have so meagerly filled their years of life: these are symptoms of their more overwhelming disease of uselessness.

Chekhov has a frugality in his writing that matches his caution with money. He was too responsible—to himself, to his family—to spend money with great abandon. This unwillingness to waste, not to get a return on something, carried over to his writing habits. He instinctively knew how to rate the exchange value of things. "While writing, I would do my best not to waste images and scenes I liked on the story at hand. Heaven knows why, but I would carefully put them away and save them for later." It is charming to think of Chekhov hoarding ideas in a spacious image bank, making measured withdrawals when he needed to.

Yalta
March 27, 1894

Greetings Alexei Sergeyevich [Suvorin]!!
 For almost a month now I've been here in Yalta, in dreariest Yalta. [. . .]
 In general, I'm in good health, but I'm ailing in several particulars. For instance, I've got a cough, an irregular heartbeat, and hemorrhoids. [. . .] Since I quit smoking for good, I am no longer at the mercy of gloomy or anxious moods. Perhaps it is due to my having given up smoking that Tolstoy's moral philosophy has lost its hold on me; in the depths of my soul I am hostile to it, which is of course unjust. I have peasant blood

flowing through my veins, so you cannot impress me with the virtues of the peasantry. Since childhood I have believed in progress, I couldn't help believing in it, because the difference between the time when they used to whip me and the time when they stopped whipping me was enormous. [. . .] But Tolstoy's philosophy had a powerful impact on me, it governed my life for six or seven years. It was not so much its basic tenets, of which I had been previously aware, as it was the Tolstoyan manner of expression, its common sense, and probably a sort of hypnotic quality. Now something within me rebels against it. Prudence and justice tell me there is more love for man in electricity and steam than in chastity and abstention from meat. [. . .] the point is that somehow or other Tolstoy has passed out of my life, he's absent from my soul, he has left me, saying, "Behold, I leave your house empty." [. . .] A person running a fever does not feel like eating, but longs for something, which he expresses by asking for "something sort of sour." I want something slightly sour too. And this is not an isolated case, for I can perceive this same mood all around me. It is as though everyone had fallen in love, had gotten over it, and now was searching for some new distraction. It is very likely that the Russian people will once more be taken by the natural sciences and materialism will become fashionable again.

My humble regards to Anna Ivanovna and the children.

A. Chekhov

LITERARY ILLUSION

The characters who populate the fictional and dramatic worlds of the work talk continuously of characters from novels, opera and plays. They philosophize about literary form, character types, styles of art; they compare themselves to fictional characters, quote lines of dialogue and descriptions from books. Chekhov, too, quoted other authors, especially in his letters, and even his own writing (a line from a story appears in a play, expressions from letters are transferred to the stage). He made fun of conventional ideas of the novel and theatre, re-imagined the possibilities of symbolism, romanticism and melodrama, and eventually discovered a new realism. One of the most stylish of writers, he was also a perceptive critic of writing which his fiction, in particular, proves.

Beyond the question of formal invention and individual taste, Chekhov's self-conscious style alludes to the real ways the art of an historical period influences, even defines, the actual lives of people living then: how they formulate experience, how they perceive art, how they frame the important questions of existence.

Chekhov created numerous characters whose knowledge of literature helps them to understand, or conveniently to misunderstand, themselves. Literature conspires with the characters to bolster their illusions: in the texts of others they discover the texts of their own lives. Ivanov understands his "Hamlet" complex, young Laevsky of "The Duel" blames his indolence and nervousness on an earlier generation of Russian writers who invented the idea of the "superfluous man" in Russian society, and the self-centered Orlov explains why he is not a "Turgenev hero" to justify his cruelty toward a lover in "An Anonymous Story." These men know themselves all too well; it has been literature, mainly, that provides the perspective. In Orlov's case, literary reference points encapsulate ironically the very real difference between the ideals of art and the realities of everyday life.

Literary illusion is more aesthetic for Zinaida, Orlov's lover, who addresses Petersburg, "I shall be even with you yet," remembering at the same time that Balzac's Pere Goriot once shouted these very words to Paris. She finds comfort in distancing her anguish of the pathetic affair and experiencing it as fiction. In a more comical vein is Solyony of *Three Sisters* who gives a performance as a Romantic hero. "But my temperament's rather like Lermontov's. I even look a little like Lermontov, I've been told—" he explains, dabbing cologne on his hands. Not the least of these humorous characters is Vanya who catches himself in his own illusions, "If I had had a normal life, I might have been a Schopenhauer, a Dostoevsky . . . Oh, I'm talking rubbish!" Throughout the plays characters quote song lyrics, poems, passages from other plays or novels when they want to evade real dialogue.

By giving his characters "literary illusions" Chekhov isolates the very complex issue of art in the making of a culture. A good part of the impetus for this technique is, of course, the opportunity for him to analyze Russian literature which he knew so well. Through his critical discourse he interrogated the texts of the past and of his own time: that is important for a writer to do. But literary quotation is also a critique of culture, a way of exploring its assumptions of style, its specific tastes, its parameters of role behavior, its power to influence individual lives. Finally, culture is the experience of art *as a country*, art being the repertoire of images in which people living in a particular time and place see themselves and their continuing history.

Art may be used as an excuse to diminish the surge of emotion through aestheticizing feelings, it may be a form of comedy to show how people manufacture their own illusions by confusing themselves with fictional types. But art as an ethical construct can also offer a truthful way to organize experience in the act of serious reflection. Chekhov's writing considers the act of literary illusion from several vantage points: the desperate need of people to make themselves up out of art and its imagined lives; the dangers of social conformity in the imitation of styles and ideas; the significant role myth has in the individual effort to invest everyday life with meaning and drama; and finally, the commendable human desire to cultivate the imagination through engagement with art.

To the doctor of "Ward No. 6" who lay dying Chekhov gave a glorious image to view in his last moments, a sentence as genteel as a string of pearls: "A herd of unusually handsome and graceful deer he had been reading about yesterday ran past him." Sometimes art becomes so great a part of human existence it cloaks the real experience of life, rendering it unutterably banal. Who can deny that to live poetically is more wonderful than any other way of life?

Melikhovo
November 11, 1896

Highly respected Anatoly Fyodorovich [Koni],
    You cannot imagine how happy your letter made me. I saw only the first two acts of my play from out front, and then I went backstage, feeling all the time that The Seagull would be a failure. The night of the performance and the following day people kept telling me that the characters I created were all idiots and that my play was dramatically awkward, ill-made, incomprehensible, nonsensical, and so on. You can imagine my situation: it was a flop exceeding my worst dreams! I was ashamed and distressed and left Petersburg full of doubts. I thought that if I had written and put on the stage a play so obviously riddled with monstrous defects, then it must mean that I had lost all sensitivity and that my mechanism had apparently broken down for good. [. . .]
    Your sincerely respectful and devoted,

A. Chekhov

ECOLOGIES OF THEATRE

Chekhov's drama stands apart from the theatre of its time to anticipate contemporary theatrical sensibility in its embrace of performance *space*, and rejection of *setting*. The more conventional notion of setting which dominated realism in Chekhov's day, and still does in our own, emphasizes the claustrophobic feel of most plays in the genre, while the idea of space comprehends the world in a yearning for freedom. It opens up to a broader view of

the individual in the world, space for the imagination to roam, already antici-
pating the new physics.

Setting entraps a play in historical time; it is mere scenery, information, the
dressing that frames a play in a set of gestures, speech styles, and moral values.
That static view of space encourages closure, pre-occupation with causality,
motivation; it is possessive of dramatic characters, reducing all their gestures to
a specific time and environment, as if there were no world beyond the fourth
wall. It separates the human being from the world, forcing the two into opposition. The concept of space, on the other hand, is dynamic, open to the world,
it allows more light in a play; it is cosmopolitan, engaged, performance-
oriented. In its three-dimensionality it assumes the attitude that human behavior has global significance and reverberates beyond the single gesture, as
ongoing narrative. All gesture, thought, language and action travel beyond the
performance space, overwhelming the idea of linear time. Space institutes a far-
ranging context for human life by reinventing the experience of time in the
drama which is transformed into a dramatic field, and this freedom brings high
definition to the nature of presence in theatrical experience. (The recent
stagings of Chekhov in this country by Andrei Serban and Lucian Pintilie succeed where the typical American ones fail precisely because they evolve in space
while the latter are bound to setting.)

In the architecture of Chekhov's dramaturgy the concept of space translates into the concept of landscape. (The complex visuality in the genre of landscape
painting developed alongside the new attitudes toward landscape Chekhov was
bringing into drama at the end of the nineteenth century. In Russia narrative
landscapes were painted by his good friend Isaak Levitan.) Now the landscape
is poetic, psychological, social, aesthetic, cultural, ontological. Chekhov invested it with moral stature, longing, propriety; he humanized it. He admired
the sensuousness of space in the body of the world, and in his feeling for it
created the real sense of people living in space, not merely against a backdrop.
Chekhov understood that the landscape has political resonance in the life of an
individual, that identity, in fact, is influenced by the experience of space: space
encompasses the livingness of all things. His spatial perspective included the
view that people make the landscape, then become part of it, so that through
the passage of time there is no separation between them. (The landscape is eter-
nal, it lives its own life.) In the history of the world the landscape as
omnipresence brings continuity to life. Chekhov in his modernity could grasp
the notion of the landscape in all its dimensions: as a marketable commodity;
as a victim of progress which brings about the displacement of human life in a
new spatial order; as a collaborator in human emotion; and finally, as a
language, a semantic space among the many languages of the world. Who first
thought of writing a play in "four acts and a landscape"?

How unexplainable that playwriting after Chekhov has almost completely ignored the implications that his great breakthrough in the conception of dramatic space as landscape suggests for the making of theatre. Only a few playwrights, namely, Gertrude Stein, Thornton Wilder, Sam Shepard, Maria Irene Fornes, Lee Breuer, Richard Foreman, Robert Wilson, and Heiner Müller have made any contribution to the new ecology of theatre. The drama of the future awaits those who will rewrite the language of subjectivity in relation to an entirely reconceived language of space. The history of theatrical space is inseparable from the transformation of the human figure.

Yalta
September 3, 1899
My dear Alexei Maximovich [Maxim Gorky], greetings once again! This is in answer to your letter.

First, I am opposed in principle to dedicating books to people who are living, whoever they may be. I used to make such dedications myself, but now I feel that perhaps I shouldn't have. This is a general observation. As to particulars, I'll be only too happy and honored to accept your dedication of Foma Gordeyev *to me. Only what did I do to deserve it? [. . .] If you can, make the wording of the dedication as simple as possible, that is, just say, "Dedicated to so and so . . ." and let it go at that.*

[. . .] Another piece of advice: when you read the galleys, take out as many adjectives and adverbs as you can. You use so many of these modifiers that the reader finds it very difficult to focus on what is important and grows tired. It is intelligible if I write, "A man sat down on the grass"—intelligible because it is clear and does not distract the reader's attention. On the other hand, it is very confusing and taxes the reader's brain unnecessarily if I write, "A tall, narrow-chested man of medium height, with a small red beard, sat down on the green grass already trampled by passers-by, doing so noiselessly and looking about timidly and fearfully." This does not convey its meaning to the reader immediately, which is what good fiction must do. [. . .]

Well, keep well. Stay alive and in good health.

Yours,
A. Chekhov

"BALZAC WAS MARRIED IN BERDICHEV"

Stanislavsky recalled that Chekhov, who was in Nice during rehearsals of *Three Sisters*, would send notes to the actors to add to or rewrite bits of dialogue. On one of these notes came Chebutykin's very funny and useless piece of knowledge that perfectly characterizes his speech style, "Balzac was married in Berdichev." If you compare Chekhov's scrap of paper with one of Sardou's, it is possible to outline two different histories of realism, one situated in language, the other in information.

THE CHEKHOVIAN ABYSS

Chekhov's characters, who always seem on the verge of beginning life over, are profoundly conscious of the lives they lead. Some long to exchange these lives, or selves, for others in order to realize the ideal visions of themselves. Others long for personal fulfillment in completely new ways of life. The three sisters are the prototypes of those characters who seek new stagings of their lives. This unsettled nature of the characters focuses the double realities operative in the worlds in which they exist. On one level, there is life as it is lived, and on the other, life as it is dreamed. The realm between the two levels of consciousness constitutes the Chekhovian abyss. It can echo laughter or tears. The typical Chekhovian character, the one who accommodates illusions, is comic. But there are also other, tragic characters who refuse the illusion in the promise of hope.

The suicides of Ivanov (*Ivanov*) and Zinaida ("An Anonymous Story") and Konstantin's attempts at it (*The Seagull*) occur because these characters are unable to perform the roles—to become the selves—they imagine they can be. They find no hope in life. They want to be other than what they are but fail in the process of transformation. Yet, their gestures toward death are respected within the ethical constructs of their world as a moral imperative, even a matter of personal choice: people own their own bodies. At other times this abyss opens to characters who choose to remain utterly what they are, and they too are triumphant in their refusal to seek simple answers to complex questions: the old professor is unable to find meaning in the world, and he will not pretend to ("A Boring Story").

Sometimes Chekhov is extraordinarily kind to his characters, and when the abyss opens up before them, he will soften the shock. So, Sonia's long speech to her uncle Vanya, so much like a sermon, even a lullaby, helps them to find salvation in the simple joy of labor. The world she imagines could only be presided over by God: Chekhov's universe is deeply Christian in its beliefs and system of rewards.

Curiously, in his plays Chekhov does not show any major characters who change their lives. Only the characters in his fiction ever succeed in this attempt. The fiction serves as the models for Chekhov's idea of performance, but the plays themselves cannot prove the success of these models of human behavior in actual life, that is, performance. This sense of failed performance is what gives the plays their expansive feeling of compassion, charity, and at times whimsy. Failure is always honorable in its aspirations to perfection, and very often humorous, too.

Yalta
March 16, 1901

Greetings, my dearest!

I am definitely coming to Moscow, but I don't know whether I'll go to Sweden this year. I'm quite tired of running around, and besides, my health is obviously becoming totally enfeebled—so you'll get in me not a husband but a grandpa. I now spend whole days digging in the garden; the weather is splendid, warm, everything's in bloom, the birds are singing, no visitors: this is what you call living. I have totally given up literature and once I marry you, I'll make you quit the stage and we'll live together like plantation owners. You're not willing to? Well, all right, go on acting some five years more and then we'll see. [. . .]

Though I have given up literature, out of sheer habit I still scribble something now and then. Right now I'm working on a story called "The Bishop"—a subject that has been running through my mind for some fifteen years. [. . .]

Write, write, my joy [. . .]

Your old Ant

THE MATTER OF LIFE AND DEATH

Who more than Chekhov presents characters so aware of their own dying? In all his work he acknowledges death—of a way of life, of a society, of friends, of feelings, of hope, of love, of pleasure, of fortitude. And yet this author, who throughout his adult writing life knew, even if he refused to believe, that he was dying of tuberculosis, projected his characters into a beautiful future. He believed in, even longed for, the future and saw in that dream the great promise for humanity.

This coda to Chekhov's writing—the plays, stories, and letters—appears again and again as theme and variation. Vershinin expresses it this way, to one of the three sisters: "So in two or three hundred years life on this old earth of ours will have become marvelously beautiful. Man longs for that, and if it isn't here yet, he must imagine it, wait for it, dream about it, prepare for it . . . "

Chekhov's visionary, utopian side pictured the individual in one great chain of being stretching to eternity. The concept of *futureness* is at the heart of his writing. It outlines his credo that one must have hope and faith in a peaceful world to come, that one must work to achieve it, simply because that is what it means to be human. Paradise for him had an earthly counterpart.

A profound meditation on death, his writing partakes of a religiosity so noble it makes all other world visions seem incomplete, vain, undignified. Who more than Chekhov has taught us moderns who deny death the most dignified way to die—first to live, then how to give up this world, and why that must be. When he was dying more than living, he wrote luxuriously of a gentle passing: *The Cherry Orchard*, his last play, alludes to the site of paradise, a garden. And in fiction of the same period he also wrote of death. For the reluctant hero of "The Bishop" death comes easy. "He just felt as if he was an ordinary simple man walking quickly and cheerfully through a field and thumping his walking-stick under a broad, sun-drenched sky. Now he was free as a bird, now he could go where he liked."

In 1904, Chekhov's death came in Badenweiler, among the trees of the Black Forest. (He loved woods more than any other staging of trees.) "I'm dying." In the last moments of his death, his wife at his side, he drank a glass of champagne. "It's been such a long time since I've had champagne." Even from Death he accepted an invitation to travel. It was yet another future.

A WRITER IN THE GARDEN

Chekhov spent so much time in his garden it is remarkable he managed to write all that he did in the last decade of his life. There were hundreds of trees and flowers to plant, ponds to dig, bushes to prune, orchards to start up. Years later when he sold his first country home and bought another, he cultivated his new land with the same necessity, all the while knowing he was dying. In his passion for life he loved the world, its luxurious body.

In the act of gardening is the essence of Chekhovian philosophy. It was through planting and caring for the land that he found another way to project himself into the future. Indeed gardening is the act in which one creates the future. In the garden one gives form to feeling, and beauty a name. Here all earthly pleasures are united in the myth of the garden of paradise, the first scene of play, its actors the first to confront the concept of future. Gardening is not simply an ecological expression but a metaphysical one as well: gardening is a way of being in the world and respecting its requests for life and death. The earth bears the seeds of new life, it cradles the dead, and we use its fertility to coax life from it. In the earth we root ourselves to the world, and to earth we return when we leave its stage. One timeless cycle of reproduction, encompassing all life and all death and all species. By his glorious example of cultivation, of himself and of his land, Chekhov offered the most profound reason to fertilize our world: others will come after us. He appreciated the world as a body to care for. He loved the face of the earth.

Gardening is a kind of writing in the landscape, and in this act Chekhov left us his language. Writing had become his way of life which he learned to live as an aesthetic experience. His signature breathes indelibly in the world in the continuous present of nature, as his commitment to humankind. How lovely to think that the pine trees he planted in Russia still stand . . . watching, crying, smiling, waiting for that wonderful future he often dreamed walking among them, cane in hand.

I shall plant these favored trees for Chekhov in my garden, and in time they too will watch and wait, his in Russia, mine in America on the other side of the world, and together, their branches clapping softly at different moments, this towering audience of pines will bear witness to countless spectacles on the earth whose fate it shares, alternately smiling and dropping acid tears.

[1984]